SHE WHO HUNTS

*Artemis: The Goddess Who
Changed the World*

CARLA IONESCU, PHD

Tellwell Talent
www.tellwell.ca

ISBN
978-0-2288-7589-5 (Hardcover)
978-0-2288-7588-8 (Paperback)
978-0-2288-7590-1 (eBook)

TABLE OF CONTENTS

Introduction 1

Chapter One
The Evolution of the Religion of Artemis 10
From Egypt to Greece: The Egyptian Transformation of
Artemis *Agrotera* 17

Chapter Two
Minoan and Mycenean Traditions: Artemis as the
Mistress of Animals 26
Artemis *Despoine*: Mistress of Mysteries 36

Chapter Three
The Embodiment of Duality: Representations of Artemis
in Greek Ritual 43
Festivals of Cakes, Fire, and Human Sacrifice 55

Chapter Four
Lady of the Wild Things 65
She Who Hunts — and Kills 88

Goddess Of Transitions: A Conclusion 104
Works Cited 108

I sing of Artemis, whose shafts are of gold, who cheers on the hounds, the pure maiden, shooter of stags, who delights in archery, own sister to Apollo with the golden sword.

Over the shadowy hills and windy peaks she draws her golden bow, rejoicing in the chase, and sends out grievous shafts.

The tops of the high mountains tremble and the tangled wood echoes awesomely with the outcry of beasts: earth quakes and the sea also where fishes shoal.

But the goddess with a bold heart turns every way destroying the race of wild beasts: and when she is satisfied and has cheered her heart, this huntress who delights in arrows slackens her supple bow and goes to the great house of her dear brother Phoebus Apollo, to the rich land of Delphi, there to order the lovely dance of the Muses and Graces.

There she hangs up her curved bow and her arrows, and heads and leads the dances, gracefully arrayed, while all they utter their heavenly voice, singing how neat-ankled Leto bare children supreme among the immortals both in thought and in deed.

- Hymn to Artemis[1]

---

[1] Anonymous. The Homeric Hymns and Homerica with an English Translation by Hugh G. Evelyn-White. Homeric Hymns. Cambridge, MA., Harvard University Press; London, William Heinemann Ltd. 1914.

INTRODUCTION

Classical Greek historians claim that the most popular Olympian deities were Apollo, Athena, Zeus, and Dionysius. The classical scholarly tradition maintains that these divinities played key roles in the communal, political, and ritual development of the Greco-Roman world. As a result, academic research on temples and ritual spaces in the Western tradition has largely focused on the validation of such claims and the continued amplification of these selected divinities.

This selective preoccupation was one of the first hurdles I had to overcome as an Artemis scholar. My research, at first, seemed as marginalized as the goddess to whom I wished to dedicate my doctoral studies. Initially, I was not sure my academic committee would even let me complete my work without "adding" another god/theme/mystery religion to my focus solely on Artemis. As a result, this work is a labour of love and the result of a little academic rebellion.

My research repeatedly shows that the deeply entrenched scholarly tradition of focusing solely on a few Olympians as the centre of Greek religion is fissured with misunderstandings of Greek and Mediterranean popular culture. In this work, I provide evidence that Artemis is in fact the most prevalent and influential deity of the Mediterranean, with roots embedded in the community and culture of this area that can be traced further back in time than even the arrival of the Greeks.

This work also demonstrates that the customs associated with the worship of Artemis were fundamental to the civic identities of her followers, not only her worship as "Virgin Huntress" but also as "Mother," "Healer" and "Saviour," and even "Death Dealer." Reverence for her was so deeply entrenched in communities across the Mediterranean that stories of her worship continue to be told by locals and tourist guides today — everywhere from Crete to Ephesus to the island of Delos, where she was famously born.

A Survey of Literature

It was extremely difficult to dig through scholarly works on archaic Greek ritual and myth only to find that Artemis had been largely ignored and set aside as a young virgin girl who loves animals and the hunt. While Homer and Herodotus did nothing to convey the influence of Artemis in Greek culture, Pausanias was able to illuminate the complexities and plethora of her worship and temples. I spent many hours tracing Pausanias' footsteps and noting every corner, seaside, and city where a temple to Artemis was once found. Pausanias cites dozens of such sites, many of which still exist today as one drives around the Peloponnese. Numerous other primary sources were also consulted in the hope of piecing together the earliest worship of Artemis and her etiology. Aeschylus, Hesiod, and Callimachus are some of the foundational primary texts when looking at the tradition of the Greek Artemis. Their writings are mostly analyzed in chapters 1 and 2. This analysis is used to establish the mythological position of Artemis in the Greek pantheon.

During the course of this research, I have come across numerous artifacts testifying to the authority, influence, and widespread worship of Artemis. It is truly astonishing that no one has put these together before. This collection of data identifies Artemis as "Parthenogenetic Mother," "Virgin," "Saviour," "Healer of All," and "Queen of Life and Death." The stories and ritual practices of the cult of Artemis all over the Mediterranean are often dismissed by scholars as remnants of mythology. I find this dismissive perspective hard to believe, however, and argue that these enduring traditions point to something more important about the actual beliefs and rites of those who worshiped and fought for Artemis, despite the introduction and influence of new cultures and religions.

While primary sources were used to identify the remnants of worship in the ancient period, secondary scholarship was consulted in order to contextualize this material. Early scholarship such as the work of Marija Gimbutas, Elinor Gadon, Rianne Eisler, and Rosemary Radford Ruether were foundational in addressing the archaeological and anthropological debates about the position of female deities in the Neolithic period (10,000–4,500 BCE). Many of the goddesses described in these texts are now viewed as archetypical and can be observed throughout history and into modern culture. The use of such texts supports my argument for the fusion of ancient mythologies with the traditions of conquering religions in the Mediterranean and modern-day Middle East. Although these authors disagree about whether or not goddesses transitioned easily within a variety of communities, most agree that some form of synthesis can be evidenced from both archeological and anthropological findings.

Ruether, for instance, maintains that although women were gatherers and agriculturists, there is no logical reason to believe that they also did not hunt or participate in other activities traditionally labelled "male." She agrees with Cynthia Eller, particularly with Eller's work in her book *Living in the Lap of the Goddess*, when she states that even if female participation in "male" activities is true, that does not automatically make these cultures matriarchal or matrifocal. And although Ruether recognizes Gimbutas as a credible archaeologist, she criticizes her suggestion that her findings from Neolithic Europe are evidence enough to create a matriarchal world ruined by patriarchal barbarians. Ruether is hesitant to rely on evidence from the early Neolithic because we simply do not have a strong understanding of ancient conceptions of religion and ritual in this period; she also criticizes Gimbutas for presenting a monotheistic "goddess culture" in this area that simply does not have any supporting evidence.[2]

Other secondary texts of Greek and Roman religious cultures focus on the development of myths and the status of religious practices and rituals within these communities. Pamela Sue Anderson's work on the significance of myth is fundamental in rethinking the importance of stories and legends in the contextualizing of culture and ritual. Anderson claims that myth is different from constitutive reason, which determines empirical knowledge. Unlike empirical knowledge, myth does not create knowledge by either compiling empirical facts or manipulating the value of words. Instead, myths are necessary in setting the limits of human knowledge and so serve a practical function. Any attempt to force myths into the role of constituting knowledge is dangerous, as it ignores the distinction between contingent knowledge and the necessary conditions of belief.[3] Myths are stories that are distinguished

[2] Ruether 2005, p. 157.
[3] Anderson 1998, p. 27.

by a high degree of constancy, and their narrative cores invite an equally pronounced capacity for marginal variation. These two characteristics make myths transmissible by tradition, and their constancy produces the attraction of recognizing them in an artistic or ritual representation.[4] That being established, it is then inadequate to merely propose that any religion can "conquer" and move against the old myths and traditions without consequence. According to Anderson, a mere reversal of power cannot confront the mythical configurations of the divine reality, especially as myths are viewed as expressions of our desires, loves, and fears, which remain part of our personal and cultural histories.[5] Again, this demonstrates the power of popular devotion — a bottom-up approach to developing theology.

Methodological Approaches

For this work, I have approached ancient and secondary texts and iconography using several methodologies, which, given the nature of what is being proposed, warrant some attention. First and foremost, I utilize the methodological approach of neo-euhemerism.[6] This means I analyze myths and legends as sources of important clues about historical events, as well as ancient cultural and cultic practices. The term *neo-euhemerism* derives from the fourth-century BCE writer Euhemerus, who investigated the actions and places of birth and burial of the divinities of popular religion, and who claimed that the gods were simply deified human beings or great heroes who were revered because they had benefited humankind in

---

[4] Ibid., p. 138.
[5] Ibid., p. 156.
[6] Rigoglioso 2009, p. 8.

some significant way. This method of interpreting Greek myth is known as *classical euhemerism*, and it was revived in the nineteenth century, particularly in the work of Martin Nilsson, whose research is fundamental to my own work. Nilsson argues that the Greek epics originated in the aristocratic society of the Mycenaean Bronze Age, and that they reflect the deeds of historical persons and describe contemporary events, mixed with mythical and folktale elements.[7] Harrison similarly argues that myth reflects broader historical contours of Greek and pre-Greek culture.[8] Farnell, too, throughout his classic five volume work, *Cults of the Greek States*, conjectures that various myths may have been indicators of actual customs and rituals.[9]

It should be noted that reading myth as history violates the assumption of those scholars who hold that myths are predominantly fictional in nature.[10] Of course, I acknowledge that myths contain fantastical elements, and that their integrity has suffered at the hands of later archaic monarchs and other influential individuals who employed such myths to suit their various needs.[11] But while myths and rituals may have been politically and culturally manipulated over time, I concur with Nilsson that they embody at least some measure of reliability, a representation of chronology, and a source of communal practice that can be used to establish the strength of belief in forming cultic relationships and bonds. Nilsson notes, "The glory and fame of ancient poets depended not, like that of modern poets, on the invention of something new and original, but rather on their presentation of the old traditional material

---

[7] Nilsson 1932, p. 196.
[8] Harrison 1903, p. 123.
[9] Farnell 1977.
[10] Dowden 1995, p. 44.
[11] Guthrie, 1967, p. 55.

in new and original fashion."[12] Thus, myths do not necessarily, or not always, exist purely in the realm of fiction but may contain genuine relics, or traces, of historical events and cultural practices.

In support of this position, Lucia Birnbaum suggests an amplified theoretical discussion of folklore as a repository for clandestine, subversive, and often subjugated and repressed religious beliefs, particularly in regard to women, the feminine, and the subaltern.[13] This theoretical claim can be expanded to include not just material found in folklore but also that which is found in the biographies of the goddesses and gods of the Greek pantheon. It is this material that is significant in establishing the importance of goddesses such as Artemis in the cultural and communal mosaic that developed in the Mediterranean for more than 2,000 years. The repetition of symbols, responsibilities, titles, and sacred spaces supports the perspective that myth and belief are initiated and established by the community and passed down from generation to generation as a form of identity and inclusivity.

Ultimately, myth and worship are a pastiche of histories, hidden codes, and politico-religious programs and propaganda and thus require multiple methods of decipherment and analysis. As a result, I do not approach the evidence from only one vantage point. Often, I apply a feminist hermeneutics of suspicion, as well as what Rigoglioso calls a "gnostic lens" — that is, viewing myths as expressions of mystical concepts corresponding with more esoteric aspects of Greek religion.[14]

This work thus begins by describing the influential nature of Artemis in the Greek world, as well as in the wider spectrum of

---

[12] Nilsson 1932, p. 2.

[13] Birnbaum 1997, pp. 3–35.

[14] Rigoglioso 2009, p. 10.

the Mediterranean world where the significance of her common worship throughout various communities can be traced. I begin by investigating Artemis' traditional role — that of the "Huntress," as she has been labelled by scholars in the field of classics — as described by Homer, Aeschylus, Plato, and other Greek writers. But the worship of Artemis as identified by these individuals is like looking at scattered pieces of a puzzle without ever putting all those pieces together. Scholars, both ancient and contemporary, have looked at Artemis' rituals, traditions, and history as individual pieces. None have put together this puzzle to see clearly that the Greek Artemis was, in fact, more influential than any other female goddess in the Olympian pantheon and almost equal to her brother Apollo in the number of her worship centres and in the wealth of her temples. This work aims to pull together all the pieces in the Artemis puzzle and present her as a complex, multilayered, multifaceted divinity who has ruled across both time and space for generations, and who continues to enchant scholars such as myself to her places of worship with her call of the wild.

Return of the Goddess Artemis
Under your Milky Way
And slow-revolving Bear,
Frogs from the alder thicket pray
In terror of your judgement day,
Loud with repentance there.

The log they crowned as king
Grew sodden, lurched and sank:
An owl floats by on silent wing,
Dark water bubbles from the spring;
They invoke you from each bank.
At dawn you shall appear,
A gaunt red-legged crane,
You whom they know too well for fear,
Lunging your beak down like a spear
To fetch them home again.

— Robert Graves[15]

[15] Graves, Robert. 1947. *Return of the Goddess Artemis*. Poetry Magazine, Vol. 71.1., pp. 22.

CHAPTER ONE

The Evolution of the Religion of Artemis

This chapter investigates the origins and development of the "early Artemis." Specifically, it traces how the religion of Artemis evolved from earlier forms of worship, from the prehistoric through to the early Christian period. Here, her primitive origins, her subjugation by the Greeks during the classical period, her continued survival through the embodiment of secondary Greek goddesses, and the proliferation of her many titles and temples found in almost every corner of the Mediterranean will be examined. As this analysis will demonstrate, the religion of Artemis was remarkably adaptive, inventive, and creative as it evolved to meet new cultural demands.

Classics textbooks and scholarly journals devote very little time to the goddess Artemis. She is typically positioned as the sister of Apollo, goddess of the hunt and "Mistress of Animals." If one were to ask the average person about the goddess Artemis, it is likely that this individual would not even recognize the name. Unlike her sister Athena, who gained notoriety not only among scholars but also among many feminist movements, both academic and spiritual, Artemis has mostly been dismissed as a secondary goddess who stood in the shade cast by her famous brother. My research will show that this is simply not the case. Not only was Artemis one of the most popular goddesses of the Mediterranean, but her rituals and places of worship are both complex and deeply rooted in pre-Greek pantheons from all over Western Europe, the Middle East, and North Africa.

Myth and ritual in ancient cultures are inseparable. As James Redfield notes, "the natives live the culture; for them myth and ritual, by explaining each other, make further explanations unnecessary."[16] This suggests that myth and ritual evolve together, and so determining which came first is rendered unnecessary. Thus, in considering the worship of Artemis, it is clear that ritual, entrenched in early pre-Greek culture, fundamentally influences her multifaceted myths — and vice versa. For Redfield, the myth is not an explanation but rather an interpretation of the ritual.[17] This means that myths are built and created not to explain the physical performance of the ritual but to interpret the psychological, emotional, and spiritual experiences of those who participate in these rites.

Rituals, or the rites of the cult, are the physical manifestations of belief. In the performance of ritual, the members of a community share not only their faith and traditions but also their shared stories or mythos. Consequently, physical participation bonds the community and allows the interpretations of myth to be modified, embellished, and transformed through each generation. This results in the phenomenon in which early rituals and myths are absorbed by later cultures. In this way, the worship of Artemis enveloped and absorbed earlier rituals

---

[16] Redfield 1990, p. 118.
[17] Ibid., p. 90.

and traditions, as well as the mythological attributes of her pre-Greek predecessors.

The religion of Artemis evolved from an early tribal and perhaps nomadic period in the Mediterranean basin. Her stories were founded in nature worship and, according to Rigoglioso, she was one of the few early parthenogenetic goddesses who evolved into representations of the divine in later Greek culture. More importantly, she is a figure whose fluidity is fundamental to her popularity, her transformations, and her prolific worship. All the rituals of Artemis described in this chapter will show evidence of some form of pre-Greek ritualistic practice. This evidence will include imagery, symbolic characteristics, and myths of origin. Since most early worship shows evidence of religions focused on orthopraxy rather than orthodoxy (that is, physical ritual practice rather than internal spiritual belief), it is easy to imagine that, for the Greeks, adapting the stories of the communities they conquered was easier than changing their communal practices.

The images, symbols, and mythos of ritual worship are foundationally significant. Conway states that "myths are used ... [because] the subconscious mind understands only symbols and pictures, not words."[18] Therefore, applying mythological tales to symbols such as the sacred trees, the wilderness, and iconic weapons such as bows and arrows assists in the transition of beliefs from one culture to another. Myths are collective stories and traditions — that is, they are shared within a specific group, and shared with outsiders. Ritual is a form of collective behaviour and evokes a specific audience.[19] We will see this practice repeated over and over in the cult of Artemis. She is a goddess with predynastic Egyptian and Minoan roots

[18] Conway 1994, p. 8.
[19] Redfield 1990, p. 119.

who was enveloped in fantastic stories told by Homer and other Greek writers, and whose prominence travelled throughout the Mediterranean and rests momentously in Ephesus.

There is clear evidence that Artemis evolved from a far more ancient and primeval period. For one, her name does not appear to be Greek, and according to Guthrie, in her early form, she was "one of the greatest, if not the greatest, of the deities worshiped by the inhabitants of pre-Hellenic Greece of western Asia minor, and of Minoan Crete."[20] He contends that the northern "barbarians" who invaded and eventually established the area now referred to as Greece had found the goddess already in place when they came to occupy the region.[21] Outsiders of a culture must integrate their communal practices with the systems of belief already in place in areas that they conquer. Consequently, the invaders, recognizing her importance, assimilated the pre-existing goddess into the Olympian pantheon as Artemis, keeping some of her foundational characteristics while embedding their own values and traditions into the already existing ritual structure.

When considering the importance of manipulating the messages and hierarchical positions of characters and events, we must consider their significance in the lives of ritual participants. As Paris notes, "Myths are complex. They do not lend themselves to dogmatic teachings. The adventures of mythic persons, gods and goddesses, are movements of consciousness; they illustrate our inter- and intra-personal conflicts, our interdependence and our participation in the sacred."[22] This shows that even though the ritual practice is a physical manifestation of communal

---

[20] Guthrie 1967, p. 99.
[21] Ibid., p. 101.
[22] Paris 1986, p. 21.

belief, the mystical relationships between the participants and the divine are also significant in the success of individual cults.

Although the works attributed to Homer are among the earliest surviving Greek texts in which Artemis plays a prominent role, she is already significantly evolved in these stories from her earlier manifestations. Farnell argues that Homer provides us with a late-stage transformation of Artemis as young maiden hunter, rather than the once powerful "Mother Goddess" of Minoan and Mycenaean religion.[23] This title harkens back to her more definitive role as an all-encompassing earth goddess. But despite this elite heritage, Homer mainly refers to her as *Potnia Theron*, or "Mistress of Animals." Under this title, he primarily positions her as the archer, the slayer of beasts, and the virgin who delights in arrows. For example, in the *Odyssey*, Homer describes Nausicaa, playing with her handmaidens after washing clothes at the shore, and he compares her to Artemis, and the epithet *io-khéaira* is used:

> [100] They threw off the veils that covered their heads and began to play at ball, while Nausicaa of the white arms sang for them. As the huntress Artemis, pourer-of-arrows [*io-khéaira*], goes forth upon the mountains of Taygetus or Erymanthos to hunt wild boars or deer, [105] and the wood-nymphs, daughters of Aegis-bearing Zeus, take their sport along with her (then is Leto proud at seeing her daughter stand a full head taller than the others, and eclipse the loveliest amid a whole bevy of beauties), even so did the untamed maiden [*parthenos*] outshine her handmaids. (*Odyssey* 6.100–109)

---

[23] Farnell 1977, v. 2, p. 427.

Hesiod, in his description of Artemis' conception and birth, also uses this epithet to define her archery skills and love of the hunt: "And Leto was joined in love with Zeus who holds the *aigis*, and bare Apollon and Artemis delighting in arrows [*io-khéaira*], children lovely above all the sons of Heaven" (*Theogony* 14.918). In the two *Homeric Hymns* dedicated to her (9 and 27), Artemis is likewise described as "she who delights in arrows," but the author does not so easily dismiss her as a huntress benefactor. Hymn 9 compliments her archery skills and her close relationship with her brother Apollo. The repetition of "delights in arrows" serves both as piety and warning:

> [1] Muse, sing of Artemis, sister of the Far-shooter, the virgin who delights in arrows, who was fostered with Apollo. She waters her horses from Meles deep in reeds, and swiftly drives her all-golden chariot through Smyrna to vine-clad Claros where Apollo, god of the silver bow, sits waiting for the far-shooting goddess who delights in arrows. And so, hail to you, Artemis, in my song and to all goddesses as well. Of you first I sing and with you I begin; now that I have begun with you, I will turn to another song. (*Hymn to Artemis* 9)

Hymn 27 repeats the above sentiment, but the emphasis here is centred on Artemis' delight in using her arrows in the chase of the hunt and the destruction of "wild beasts":

> [1] I sing of Artemis, whose shafts are of gold, who cheers on the hounds, the pure maiden, shooter of stags, who delights in archery, own sister to Apollo with the golden sword. Over

the shadowy hills and windy peaks [5] she
draws her golden bow, rejoicing in the chase,
and sends out grievous shafts. The tops of the
high mountains tremble and the tangled wood
echoes awesomely with the outcry of beasts:
earth quakes and the sea also where fishes shoal.
But the goddess with a bold heart [10] turns
every way destroying the race of wild beasts: and
when she is satisfied and has cheered her heart,
this huntress who delights in arrows slackens her
supple bow and goes to the great house of her
dear brother Phoebus Apollo, to the rich land
of Delphi, [15] there to order the lovely dance
of the Muses and Graces. There she hangs up
her curved bow and her arrows, and heads and
leads the dances, gracefully arrayed, while all
they utter their heavenly voice, singing how
neat-ankled Leto bare children [20] supreme
among the immortals both in thought and in
deed. Hail to you, children of Zeus and rich-
haired Leto! And now I will remember you and
another song also. (*Hymn to Artemis* 27)

We see here a hunter that slays animals in the forest rather
than a goddess who protects them. The author has created a
fearsome figure who is categorically removed from her role as
"Mistress of Animals" and protector of the mountains, but who
delights, rather, in the killing of wild beasts and returns to take
her seat next to her male counterpart, her brother Apollo. There
she dances and celebrates her mother Leto with the Muses
and Graces, all the while putting up her bow and arrows to
reign supreme among the Olympic immortals. While this view

of Artemis is embedded in Greek patriarchal thought, much of her ancient roots as "Mistress of Animals" and a powerful goddess in her own right has been reimagined to allow her a smooth transition into the Olympian family. As we will see in the following section, this supports both Rigoglioso's and Farnell's claims that Artemis' more primitive aspects have been assimilated under the guise of "sister" and "leader of nymphs."

From Egypt to Greece: The Egyptian Transformation of Artemis *Agrotera*

As Artemis *Agrotera*, "the Huntress," the goddess is often described in association with the wilderness, with nature, but particularly with her bow and arrow. As mentioned above, Homer often identifies her as the goddess who loves archery and the slaying of beasts. Unlike her Ephesian counterpart, who stands between two lions, the Greek Artemis is often painted and/or sculpted wearing a quiver of arrows and attended by a stag or several dogs. The mountains, rivers, and groves are her sanctuary, and she can be both unforgiving and merciful. Her lack of a male companion and her violently guarded chastity make her the prime incarnation of traditions that trace their roots to predynastic Egypt.

Artemis *Agrotera* seems to have evolved from two Egyptian deities: (1) Neith, "Mistress of the Bow and Ruler of the Arrows," a goddess whose primordial existence is embedded in Egyptian thought, and (2) Bastet (also known as Bast, Pasht, and Bubastis), the cat goddess who delights in dancing and music and is representative of the moon, marriage, and motherhood.

Neith: Mistress of Arrows

Neith was one of the oldest of all the Egyptian deities and one of the most important divinities during the early historic period.[24] I contend that Artemis inherited many of the attributes and traits traditionally associated with Neith, particularly her weapons and aspects of her imagery worship, as part of her pre-Greek heritage. There is strong evidence that Neith's worship was widespread in predynastic times.[25] Near the beginning of the First Dynasty (c. 2920–2770 BCE), Aha, the first historical king of Egypt, dedicated a temple to her at Sais,[26] and her emblem of crossed bows appears on some decorated pottery as early as the last phase of the predynastic period (c. fourth millennium BCE.).[27] That Neith was widely worshiped in the earliest dynastic period and enjoyed a prominent role in the Egyptian royal court is evident from the fact that nearly forty per cent of dynastic personal names incorporate her name, including four royal women of the First Dynasty, two of them clearly queens and related to the first three dynastic kings.[28]

A text from the Ramesside period of the New Kingdom (c. 1304–1075 BCE) affirms that Neith was held to be the "great and divine Mother" in primeval times, and she is said to have mediated the dispute between Horus and Seth for divine kinship.[29] In dynastic times, she was the most important goddess, and possibly the most important divinity in general, of the Northern Kingdom. Her cult reached its height during the

---

[24] Rigoglioso 2009, p. 26.
[25] Budge 1915, v. 1, p. 450; Hollis 1994–5, p. 46.
[26] Emery 1961, p. 51.
[27] Petrie 1901, pl. 20 no. 11; Adams 1988, p. 51.
[28] Rigoglioso 2009, p. 27.
[29] Lichtheim 1973, v. 2, p. 215.

Old Kingdom at Sais (c. 2525–2134 BCE) but continued to be important in the Middle and New Kingdoms.[30]

According to Kees, in the Old Kingdom, the Egyptians characterized this goddess as "Neith from Libya, as if she were the chieftaness of this neighboring people with whom the inhabitants of the Nile Valley were at all times at war."[31] Herodotus and other Greek writers saw her as originating in Libya as well, which was the Greek designation for all of North Africa to the west and southwest of Egypt.

Neith's symbolic image is a pair of crossed arrows, sometimes laid over a shield-like sign. Rigoglioso claims that this image is the equivalent of a similar symbol found in the predynastic period, thus suggesting its great antiquity.[32] In her anthropomorphic form, Neith frequently holds in her hand a bow and two arrows, and in later times she was called "Mistress of the Bow and Ruler of the Arrows."[33] Such symbolism may indicate that Neith was originally the goddess of war, or the goddess of the hunt, but there is little mythological evidence to support this theory.[34] Clearly, however, the symbol of the bow and arrow has been handed down to Artemis, which have become the goddess's most identifiable weapons. Along with the title of "Mistress," Artemis inherits the attributes of this Egyptian goddess, both in her depictions as well as her demeanor.

One Egyptian text speaks of Neith as having set her arrow to her bow and slaying all her enemies,[35] and in funerary contexts, Neith is often depicted as shooting arrows at evil spirits to

---

[30] Rigoglioso 2009, p. 27.

[31] Kees 1961, p. 28.

[32] Ibid., p. 28.

[33] Lesko 1999, p. 46.

[34] Rigoglioso 2009, p. 27.

[35] Budge 1915, v. 1, p. 462.

protect the deceased.[36] Herodotus (*Histories* 4.180) confirms that Neith was worshiped by the Libyan (Ause) tribe of his day, and that this worship involved a combat ritual among the tribes' maidens. Although Artemis does not slay evil spirits, she is famous for setting her bow and arrow and slaying those who offend the gods, as well as those who break her rules of chastity and privacy. Moreover, that Auses, according to Herodotus, is a location that has been identified as contemporary Tunisia indicates that, at least in the Greek Classical period, the worship of this goddess extended well past the borders of western Egypt.

The evolution of Artemis from Neith is also evident in Homer, where he primarily refers to Artemis as *Potnia Theron*, "Mistress of Animals," or *Agrotera*, "Huntress" or "Goddess of the Wilderness" (e.g., *Iliad* 21.470). Just like Neith, Artemis "draws her golden bow … [and] the tops of the high mountains tremble and the tangled wood echoes awesomely with the outcry of beasts" (*Hymn to Artemis* 27). Aeschylus similarly refers to her as "Mistress Maiden" (*Despoina Nymphê*), ruler of the stormy mountains" (frag. 188, from Orion, *Etymologicum* 26.5), and a line from the Homeric *Hymn to Aphrodite* (5.16) describes Artemis "Of the Golden Distaff" (*Khryselakatos*) and praises her "love of archery and the slaying of wild beasts in the mountains."

There is a fearsomeness in her "love of archery," both from an athletic, physical perspective, but also from the severity of using a bow and arrow to destroy and/or protect. For thousands of years, hunting was the primary means of subsistence for small bands and, later, hunting weapons were used to protect a community's farms. As such, Artemis is more than just a maiden of the woods; she is a symbol of human survival, ingenuity, skill, and the ability to protect those under one's care.

---

[36] Sayed 1982, pp. 81–85.

These complimentary characteristics of protection and survival suggest that Artemis is the Greek interpretation of the Egyptian Neith. Her label as "the Huntress" and her use of arrows to punish offenses and protect those under her care show a direct correlation between Egyptian tradition and Greek myth. The similarity in imagery plus the overlapping of attributes between the Egyptian Neith and the Greek Artemis provide overwhelming evidence that Artemis is the inheritor and/or direct descendant of this very ancient tradition.

Bastet: The Frenzy-Loving Goddess

At Bubastis, Artemis is popularly connected to the Egyptian goddess Bastet, also known as Pasht or Bast. Bastet is the counterpart of Hathor (the goddess of motherhood) and similarly delights in dancing and music. Her head is that of a cat and she is usually represented with a cistern of dancing women in her hand and a basket in her arms. When these secondary characteristics are omitted, however, it is difficult to distinguish between her and the goddess Sekhmet ("the mighty one"), who has the head of a lion.[37] Adolf Erman notes that Egyptians found a connection between these two goddesses and their two animals: "For even though Sekhmet is a terrible goddess of war and strife, the question arises whether both of these divinities did not develop originally from such a sky goddess as Neith."[38] Bastet was also worshiped all over Lower Egypt, but her cult was centred in her temple at Bubastis, which is now in ruins. Bubastis was the capital of ancient Egypt for a time during the Late Period, and several pharaohs included the goddess Bastet in their royal names.

---

[37] Erman 1907, pp. 13–14.
[38] Ibid., p. 16.

As "Mistress of Animals," Artemis is often represented standing between two lions, particularly in Ephesus. The cat/lion representation is especially significant because of the animal's connection to the moon. Plutarch makes this connection by describing the cat as a "fickle, nocturnal, prolific animal, [which] widens its eyes at the full moon" (*Isis and Osiris* 63). Artemis is often referred to as the goddess of the moon, and whether she inherits this title from her Egyptian heritage, or this name was granted to her due to her overlap with Hecate and Selene, she remains intrinsically connected to her Egyptian roots.

Herodotus tells us that "the Egyptians hold solemn assemblies not once a year, but often. The principal one of these and the most enthusiastically celebrated is that in honour of Artemis at the town of Bubastis" (*Histories* 2.59). Each year on the day of her festival, the town is said to have attracted some 700,000 visitors, both men and women (but not children), who arrive in numerous crowded ships. The women engage in music, song, and dance, and they drink wine on their way to the temple, where great sacrifices were made in Artemis' honour. This accords well with Egyptian sources, which prescribe that leonine goddesses are to be appeased with "feasts of drunkenness."[39] The worship of Artemis at times includes festivals of wild and "drunken" behaviour. She is often the divine counterpart of Dionysus and described as the frenzy-loving goddess.[40] Her love of dancing, racing, and competition, as well as the wildness and freedom of the natural realm, make her a fitting vessel for the Egyptian Bastet.

There are several times where Herodotus refers to Aeschylus, who identified Artemis with Bastet and Apollo with Horus; Aeschylus also identified Leto with the Egyptian goddess Uto

[39] Velde 1999, pp. 164–165.
[40] Downing 1996, p. 179.

(*Histories* 2.155). According to this legend, Apollo and Artemis are still brother and sister, but their parents are Dionysus, represented as Osiris, and Isis. In this version, Leto (Uto) is made into the siblings' nurse and preserver (*Histories* 2.156). The tradition of Artemis as Bastet is well documented into the second century CE. Pausanias claims that "Artemis [the Egyptian goddess Bastet] was the daughter, not of Leto but of Demeter [Egyptian Isis] which is the Egyptian account"(8.37.6). This is later confirmed by Antoninus Liberalis in his *Metamorphoses*:

> Typhon felt an urge to usurp the rule of Zeus and not one of the gods could withstand him as he attacked. In panic they fled to Aegyptus [Egypt] …. When they fled, they had changed themselves in anticipation into animal forms … Artemis [became] a cat [i.e., the Egyptian goddess Bastet]. (Antoninus Liberalis, *Metamorphoses* 28)

These traditions allow us to see the ancient implications of the worship of Artemis and her primeval connections with the territory of North Africa.

The evidence provided in the Egyptian traditions of Neith and Bastet supports my conclusion that Artemis has far more complex roots then previously considered by scholars. She inherits her bow and arrow, her sense of justice and protection, and her elite status as *Potnia Thea*, or "Goddess Queen," from the tradition of Neith. In addition, it is also clear that she inherits her wild and carefree attributes, as well as her preference for the natural realm, from the tradition of Bastet. But the worship of Artemis is much more convoluted and widespread than her Egyptian roots alone would suggest. The mantle of her inheritance reaches deep into Minoan traditions and further into the Mycenaean world. In the next chapter, we will look at how Artemis represents the fundamental figure through which ancient Minoan divinities survive, despite being conquered and/ or married off to the gods of the Greeks.

Prais'd be Diana's Fair and Harmless Light
BY SIR WALTER RALEGH
Prais'd be Diana's fair and harmless light;
Prais'd be the dews wherewith she moists the ground;
Prais'd be her beams, the glory of the night;
Prais'd be her power by which all powers abound.

Prais'd be her nymphs with whom she decks the woods,
Prais'd be her knights in whom true honour lives;
Prais'd be that force by which she moves the floods;
Let that Diana shine which all these gives.

In heaven queen she is among the spheres;
In aye she mistress-like makes all things pure;
Eternity in her oft change she bears;
She beauty is; by her the fair endure.

Time wears her not: she doth his chariot guide;
Mortality below her orb is plac'd;
By her the virtue of the stars down slide;
In her is virtue's perfect image cast.

A knowledge pure it is her worth to know:
With Circes let them dwell that think not so.

- Sir Walter Raleigh[41]

---

[41] "Prais'D Be Diana'S Fair And Harmless Light By Sir Walter Raleigh. 1593. | Poetry Foundation". *Poetry Foundation*, 2022,

CHAPTER TWO

Minoan and Mycenean Traditions: Artemis as the Mistress of Animals

The connection between Artemis and the Minoan "Mistress of Animals" has been supported by scholars for the last forty years. She has also been associated with goddesses such as Cybele, Hecate, Selene, and other lesser known or unnamed divinities, particularly on the island of Crete. Her inheritance of the symbols, rituals, and attributes of the Minoan goddess of nature will be evidenced here. Marinatos claims that after the collapse of the Mycenaean world at the end of the Bronze Age, the Dorians were met with a fragmented set of deities whom they recast according to their own religious beliefs and social institutions.[42] However, many of the Dorians' fundamental beliefs and ritual practices, along with the goddess they primarily worshiped, survived well into the Greek Classical period. The "Mistress of Animals," who often appears in the role of Huntress, armed with a bow or spear,[43] can be easily identified with the earliest descriptions of Artemis as *Iokheaira*

[42] Marinatos 1993, p. 12.
[43] Nilsson 1971, *Minoan-Mycenaean Religion*, p. 389.

"Of Showering Arrows" (Homer, *Iliad* 9.538) or *Khryselakatos* "Of the Golden Distaff"" who "Delights in Arrows" (*Hymn to Artemis* 9.1). And although most scholars agree that the Minoan "Mistress of Animals" is directly linked to the Greek "Mistress of Animals," some components of both the character of the goddess and the rituals of her cultic worship require further analysis.

Both the divine nature and function of the "Mistress of Animals" show that Artemis is of Minoan origin. Nilsson notes that "Artemis is not the goddess of Classical mythology, the sister of Apollo, but a ruder and more primitive type of deity which was widespread especially in the Peloponnesus and among the Dorian peoples; she is in fact the most popular goddess of Greece, at least in the cult of the simple rustic people."[44] This Artemis is the goddess of wild nature who is not touched or altered by the hands of men. She roams the mountains and forests, and in the shadowy groves and wet meadows she hunts and dances together with her nymphs, who have faith in her as their fearless protector. In fact, dances are very common in her cult. These dances are of an orgiastic and at times indecent character, and the dancers are often depicted wearing masks. Such scenes do not fit with the Greek tradition of Artemis as a virgin goddess. In tandem with this, the Minoan goddess is never shown inside a shrine. She manifests herself within a natural environment seated under a tree or on a rock.[45] Pausanias claims that in "Dereion [in Lacedaemonia], there is in the open an image of Artemis *Dereatis*, and beside it is a spring which they name *Anonos*, [and] when Artemis cannot be worshipped, [a representation of] her temple is often erected in a grove or near a natural spring" (3.20.7). Further to her worship, which

---

[44] Ibid., p. 503.
[45] Marinatos 1993, p. 160.

is often established in a grove or near a natural spring, Artemis is also specifically associated with the worship of trees.

In addition to the shared characteristics between Artemis and the Minoan "Mistress of Animals," Nilsson further suggests that the worship of Artemis contains remnants of another equally popular Minoan divinity, the goddess of nature. The Minoan nature goddess was a goddess of fertility — not of agrarian fertility, but of the fertility of humans and animals. She helped females bring forth their young and assisted women in the pangs of childbirth, fostering young animals and children alike. She is also intimately connected with one form of the tree cult, established around the sacred Bo tree, which conveys life and fertility.[46] Artemis inherits many of the same characteristics: she is a goddess of fertility, particularly in her Ephesian incarnation, she helps women in childbirth, and she is often worshiped in the guise of a tree. Pausanias, for example, describes her worship as a myrtle tree in Boeae, a village in Lacedaemonia, as follows: "They built a city on the site of the myrtle, and down to this day they worship that myrtle tree, and name Artemis *Sôteira* [Saviour]" (3.22.12). Nilsson notes that there is a close connection between the goddess of the tree cult and the "Mistress of Animals"; both being nature goddesses, it would not be unnatural to regard them as forms of the same deity.[47] Consequently, Artemis inherits the attributes of the "Mistress of Animals," whose close associations with other Minoan goddesses of nature would also be inherited. Here again we see her embodying the imagery, weapons, responsibilities, and attributes of her earlier counterparts. This provides further evidence that Artemis is not a divinity created by the Greeks as part of their pantheon but was a goddess already deeply rooted

---

[46] Nilsson 1971, *Minoan-Mycenaean Religion,* p. 389.

[47] Ibid., p. 399.

in earlier Minoan and Mycenaean traditions, who was more easily transfigured into a goddess that could be categorized as Greek rather than removed outright.

To further substantiate this claim, we will look at two popular Minoan goddesses whose attributes became fundamental in the Greek worship of Artemis: Eileithyia, whose main role is as protector and nurse, and Britomartis, whose chastity and ferocious protection of her virginity become an emblematic factor in the myths and culture of Artemis' worship.

Artemis as Minoan Eileithyia: She Who Comes to Aid

Eileithyia seems to be a name for one form of the Minoan nature goddess, and it is probable that the Homeric tradition derives from the Minoan age.[48] Pausanias supports her pre-Greek roots by referring to the earlier Lycian poet Olen, who wrote a hymn to Eileithyia in which he described her as "the clever spinner," identifying her with Fate and making her older than Cronus (Pausanias 8.21.3). Pausanias also confirms that she was born in the cave at Amnisos, and that Hera was her mother (Pausanias 1.18.5). Nilsson's discussion of the archeological findings at the cave to Eileithyia in Amnisos supports the tradition that this is the location where, according to Homer, Odysseus once anchored his boat (*Odyssey* 19.188). Thus, a cult to Eileithyia can clearly be traced back as far as the Minoan period.

Initially, Homer describes this goddess in plural form: "The hard *Eileithyiai* ("Spirits of Childbirth") ... Hera's daughters, who hold the power of the bitter birth pangs" (*Iliad* 11.270). The later Roman author Aelian also uses a plural form when describing "the *Eileithyiai*" (*On Animals* 7.15); however, the

---

[48] Marinatos 1993, p. 165.

goddess is elsewhere depicted as one female deity, and often, she is merged with Artemis. In fact, according to at least one early writer, Artemis and Eileithyia share the same mother. Nonnus writes that "she [Aura] hated Artemis and would not call upon her in her pains; she would not have the daughters of Hera [the *Eileithyiai*], lest they as being children of [Bacchus'] stepmother should oppress her delivery with more pain" (*Dionysiaca* 48.794). This might explain the plural use of Eileithyia's name and her overlapping worship as Artemis.

According to Hesiod, Eileithyia is one of the three children Zeus and Hera conceived together "out of love" (*Theogony* 921). Her name means "she who comes to aid" or "relieve" from the Greek word *elêluthyia*. Her Roman counterpart was Natio ("Birth") or Lucina ("Light-Bringer"). She is often depicted as Artemis, or alongside Artemis, such as here in the *Orphic Hymns*: "When racked with labour pangs, and sore distressed, the sex invoke thee [Artemis Eileithyia], as the soul's sure rest; for thou Eileithyia alone canst give relief to pain, which art attempts to ease, but tries in vain. Artemis Eileithyia, venerable power, who bringest relief in labour's dreadful hour" (*Orphic Hymn* 2). In addition to being the goddess of childbirth, she also assists all animals in procreation and labour: "In spring the *Eileithyiai* deliver most part of the fishes from the heavy travail of spawning ... not even on the fishes have the *Moirai* [Fates] bestowed easy birth, and not alone to women upon earth are their pains, but everywhere the birth-pangs are grievous" (Oppian, *Halieutica* 1.476). Clearly, this is a tradition that can be traced through the popular evolution of Artemis as assistant in childbirth.

Although there are conflicting details, Eileithyia's presence is fundamental in the account of the birth of Heracles. The Homeric tradition has Eileithyia helping Alcmene deal with premature labour set upon her by a jealous Hera (Homer, *Iliad* 19.103). Later traditions claim that, in fact, Eileithyia, as a favour to her jealous mother, is responsible for initiating the premature labour and for keeping Alcmene in labour pains. Diodorus Siculus writes that

> Zeus, whose mind was fixed upon the birth of [Heracles], announced in advance in the presence of all the gods that it was his intention to make the child who should be born that day king over the descendants of Perseus; whereupon Hera, who was filled with jealousy, using as her helper Eileithyia her daughter, checked the birth-pains of [Alcmene] and brought Eurystheus forth to the light before his full time. (Diodorus Siculus 4.9.4)

Either way, Eileithyia plays a crucial role in the birth and survival of Heracles, who is one of Zeus' favoured human sons.

Interestingly, Eileithyia is also responsible for the successful, and *single*, birth of Zeus' most favoured divine son, Apollo. This tradition, preserved in the Homeric *Hymn to Delian Apollo*, claims that Leto, pregnant with Apollo, went into labour on the island of Delos. Leto suffered through nine days and nights of labour pangs, and although other goddesses crowded around her, none could ease her pains. The goddesses sent out Iris to bring Eileithyia, promising her a great necklace strung with golden threads, nine cubits long. As soon as Eileithyia set foot on Delos, the pains of birth seized Leto, and she was ready to give birth to Apollo. Leto wrapped her arms around a palm tree and the child leaped forth to the light. This becomes particularly important when we consider Artemis as Virgin Mother. According to Rigoglioso, Artemis comes from a matriarchal line of pre-Greek

31

goddesses that were involved in parthenogenetic conception.[49] Rigoglioso also asserts that "the Apollonian element was a later insertion into what was originally a pre-Greek story depicting matriarchal consciousness."[50] This point of view of matrilineal ancestry shows that Artemis is more likely the sister of Leto, or the partner of Leto, rather than her daughter. According to this tradition, Artemis is not even present at her "twin" brother's birth. In fact, there is no sister or any other sibling mentioned in this account. This connects to Rigoglioso's suggestion that Artemis was a primordial goddess whose worship survived into the Hellenistic period, but who originally played the role of Virgin Mother and governed all life cycles rituals for both her male and female worshippers. Through her worship as Artemis Eileithyia, she encompasses all attributes of "Protector." In this role, she is the helper, the "Saviour," the great "Mother Goddess," and guardian of all those who ask for her mercy.

Traditionally, the argument is that Artemis takes on the mantle of Eileithyia and absorbs her attributes, specifically the role of "Protector." However, the evolution of Artemis is much more complex. I suggest that Artemis was the only possible goddess who could have absorbed these characteristics of Eileithyia due to her already expansive inheritance from the "Mistress of Animals" and the Minoan goddess of nature. Artemis is the only logical deity who could carry all the above roles without compromising the quality and morality of ritual worship. In addition, if she is a parthenogenetic goddess or Virgin Mother, as Rigoglioso claims, it makes sense that she is not born of Leto but assists her in birthing Apollo as Eileithyia. The tradition of Artemis being the first to jump out of Leto's womb and then assist in the birth of her brother is clearly a

---

[49] Rigoglioso 2009, p. 54.
[50] Ibid., p. 55.

post-Homeric addition. This addition is further evidence of Artemis' continuous transformation and adaptation: She is the medium through which the members of the community maintain their ritual practices while allowing some modification to their mythological interpretation. Artemis is the vessel into which all goddess-related images and attributes come to be placed.

The Story of Minoan Britomartis: Artemis Inherits Virginal and Vengeful Attributes

Another interesting incarnation of Artemis that is woven through the Minoan pantheon is the tradition of Britomartis. Her name is usually derived from *britus*, meaning "sweet" or "blessing," and *martis* or *marna*, meaning "maiden," so that her name comes to mean "the sweet or blessing maiden" (Pausanias 3.14.2). Britomartis, who is sometimes called Dictynna, was born at Caino on Crete. Her parents are Zeus and Carme, the daughter of Euboulos, who was the son of Demeter. She invented the *diktya*, "nets," used in hunting, which is why she is sometimes called Dictynna, and she is later seen passing her time in the company of Artemis (Diodorus Siculus 5.76.3). Similar in their communal worship, Britomartis and Artemis were merged into the same goddess over time.[51]

The intricacies with which these two goddesses are blended are phenomenal. Callimachus, in his *Hymn to Artemis*, describes Britomartis as "the goodly archer" who escapes the advances of King Minos of Crete for nine months by hiding under oak trees and in the meadows (*Hymn to Artemis* 188). According to Strabo,

---

[51] Conway 1994, p. 33. According to Conway, Britomartis (or Dictynna), as an ancient Cretan form of a virgin huntress, may well have been the original form of Artemis.

when Minos continued to pursue her, she leapt into fishermen's nets (*Geography* 10.4.12). Britomartis and Artemis were the first to hold quivers on their shoulders, and according to at least one account, on their right shoulders they wore the quiver strap and "always the right breast showed bare" (Callimachus, *Hymn to Artemis* 188).

Britomartis, like Artemis, is also "ever-virgin" and thus described as the "most loved" of Artemis' hunting companions (Callimachus, *Hymn to Artemis* 190–191). Nonnus describes her as "love-shy Britomartis" (*Dionysiaca* 33.332), while other accounts of her guarded maidenhead are almost identical to that of Artemis: "Zeus made love to [Carme] and fathered Britomartis who avoided the company of mankind and yearned to be a virgin for always" (Antoninus Liberalis, *Metamorphoses* 40). It is because of this self-imposed chastity that she hides from Minos and avoids all male attention. As they share similar moralities and attributes, and Britomartis passes most of her time in the company of Artemis, it stands to reason that many communities worshiped them as the same goddess, for whom they built temples and sacrificed in the same locations (Diodorus Siculus 5.76.3). This overlapping association of ever-virgin is both what endears Britomartis to Artemis, but also alludes back to a more ancient past, when as Rigoglioso claims, powerful goddesses were parthenogenetic and chose to remain untouched by men.[52]

As we have seen, Diodorus Siculus states that Britomartis was known as Dictynna, "she of the nets," because she invented the net used in hunting (5.76.3). Aristophanes, however, gives credit for this invention to Artemis by referring to her by the name Dictynna: "O Artemis, thou maid divine, Dictynna, huntress, fair to see" (Aristophanes, *Birds* 1358). The Orphic

---

[52] Rigoglioso 2009, p. 51.

Hymn to Artemis also refers to her as "torch-bearing Goddess, Dictynna divine" (*Orphic Hymn* 36), and Apuleius names her the "arrow-bearing Dictynna Diana" (*The Golden Ass* 11.5). This shows an intriguing cross-sectionality in titles and responsibilities between these two divinities. Even in Sparta, where the cult of Artemis *Limnaie*, "of the lake," is deeply ingrained in the community, she is recognized as Britomartis of Crete (Pausanias 3.14.2). Consequently, we can clearly see a correlation between imagery in myth, cult association, and ritual. It is easy to see why Artemis and Britomartis are often considered the same divinity. It is also part of the pattern that surrounds the ritual practice and worship of Artemis.

This pattern of worship has provided us with evidence of the ancient and widespread roots of Artemis' veneration. As the evolution of the worship of Artemis shows, she is the bridge between the Greeks and the pre-Greek civilizations of the Mediterranean. She embodies an inheritance of many rituals and responsibilities of her pre-Greek divine collaborators. She is the carrier of the divine feminine, and her celestial will is expressed through blood, ritual, and sacred tradition. In chapter 1, we identified that some of her characteristics come from Egyptian traditions — qualities such as her weaponry and her protection of the weak (the young, the old, animals, etc.), as well as attributes such as her love for dancing and competition, her playfulness, and her love for the wilderness in nature. Then, in the first part of this chapter, we discussed her Minoan and Mycenaean heritage. From these traditions we have seen her inherit the role of nurse and caregiver — she who eases pain — as well as the adoption of her attitude towards virginity, her severe chastity, and her custom of having numerous female followers and nymphs. Taken together, this has provided clear evidence that Artemis is the sole surviving deity after the Greeks conquered most of the Mediterranean. Her embodiment of these numerous qualities is clearly an attempt by the already existing, or native community, to keep their indigenous practices and rituals within their group. Consequently, Artemis carries the mantle of her earlier companions into Greek culture and is therefore one of the sole links to the prehistory of this region. Her survival is the key to understanding how ritual practice affects communities, their histories, and their beliefs.

Artemis *Despoine*: Mistress of Mysteries

An analysis of the goddess Despoine ("Mistress"), the mysterious and unnamed daughter of Demeter, the predynastic Egyptian goddess Neith ("Mistress of the Bow and Ruler of the Arrows"), and the Minoan "Mistress of Animals" all points directly to the worship of Artemis. Having been gifted with the term "Mistress" while inheriting the mantle of responsibility from her prehistoric past, it is logical that we find Artemis associated with the most mysterious of Greek goddesses. Since the mystery goddess only carries the title "Mistress," I argue that she is the incarnation of an older parthenogenetic female divinity tied to the land from a far more ancient period, when goddesses were imagined as dual, or as one half of an equal partnership.

The sanctuary of Despoine is in Arcadia. According to Pausanias, this sanctuary housed a temple with a bronze image of Artemis *Hegemone* ("Leader"), and from this temple there was an entrance into the sacred enclosure of Despoine. In the same passage, the mystery of Despoine is described by Pausanias as follows:

> Those about the sanctuary say that Despoine was brought up by Anytos, who was one of

the Titans [perhaps here Curetes], as they are
called … This is the story of Anytos told by
the Arcadians. That Artemis was the daughter,
not of Leto but of Demeter, which is the
Egyptian account, the Greeks learned from
[Aeschylus] the son of Euphorion. Despoine
became worshipped in a sanctuary at Lycosura
west to the town of Megalopolis. This is a
very important site for the study of ancient
mystery religions, although this cult remained
regional rather than Panhellenic. (Pausanias
8.37.6–38.2)

The correlation between Artemis and Despoine is layered under
the many transmutations of Egyptian and Minoan goddesses
who wear the mantle of "Mistress." Nilsson argues that "the
connections of Minoan Crete with Egypt were closer than
those with any other country, and to this fact due regard must
also be taken when dealing with religion."[53] Consequently,
it is extremely probable that a natural evolution from Egypt
to Minoan Crete to Greece would take place through the
community of worshippers of Artemis.

It is no coincidence that Pausanias finds multiple
representations of Artemis in the sanctuary of Despoine in
Arcadia. Her impressive bronze statue in front of the entrance to
the mystery cult stood at least six feet tall (Pausanias 8.37.1), and
inside the sacred sanctuary by the side of the statue of Demeter
stood another statue of Artemis "wrapped in the skin of a deer,
and carrying a quiver on her shoulders, while in one hand she
holds a torch, in the other two serpents" (Pausanias 8.37.1).
Artemis plays a fundamental part in this mystery religion, and

---

[53] Nilsson 1971, *Minoan-Mycenaean Religion*, p. 9.

it is clear through the physical position of her temple statues that she is either the unnamed daughter of Demeter, or her equal.

Kerenyi supports the claim that the cult of Despoine was a continuation of an early cult of a Minoan goddess.[54] His connection is supported by material evidence from the Minoan and Mycenaean periods. In the mysteries, Demeter was viewed as a second goddess under her daughter, Despoine. The myths were connected with the first Greek-speaking people who came from the north during the Bronze Age. The two goddesses had close connections with the rivers and the springs and were related to the god of rivers and springs, Poseidon, and especially with Artemis, who was the first nymph. The concept of partnership between two goddesses has both Minoan and Egyptian roots. In Egypt, Neith is often part of or paralleled to Hathor, who in turn is often part of or paralleled to Bast, who herself was often part of or parallel to Sekhmet. This union of two goddesses whose characteristics complement each other has deeply ancient roots. In Minoan religion, this complementary relationship between two goddesses also exists. The Hagia Triada Sarcophagus (c. 1400 BCE), for example, depicts two reliefs that partner up two female deities.[55] The goddesses depicted on the sarcophagus riding in a goat-drawn chariot are mirrored by the two goddesses in the griffin-drawn chariot. Marinatos notes that the two pairs are counterparts to each other; two chthonic goddesses paralleled to two celestial goddesses.[56] Therefore, the coupling of Demeter and Despoine has widespread pre-Greek origins in material culture and imagery.

Despoine's epithet as "Mistress" is the fundamental feature that connects her to early goddesses, as well as to Artemis. The

---

[54] Kerenyi 1967, p. 88.
[55] Marinatos 1993, p. 36.
[56] Ibid., p. 37.

Minoan goddess is titled the "Mistress of Animals," and, as mentioned above, the term "Mistress" is also commonly used in reference to the Egyptian goddess Neith. Moreover, Aeschylus refers to Artemis as "Mistress Maiden" (*Despoina Nymphê*), who is ruler of the stormy mountains (frag. 188), and, more convincingly, the Arcadians have a mountain called Cnacalus "where every year they celebrate mysteries in honour of their Artemis" (Pausanias 8.23.3). On his travels, Pausanias also finds additional places where Demeter, "her daughter," and Artemis have been long worshipped together: "On the citadel [at Phlious, Sicyonia] is another enclosure, which is sacred to Demeter, and in it are a temple and statue of Demeter and her daughter. Here there is also a bronze statue of Artemis, which appeared to me to be ancient" (Pausanias 2.13.5). Nilsson contends that Artemis is akin to an especially Arcadian type of goddess, or rather, a pair of goddesses, who are for this reason also identified with Demeter and Kore (Persephone).[57] The Arcadians referred to these goddesses as the "Mistress" (*Despoine*) or the "Saviour" (*Sôteira*). These were said to be very strange beings; the garment of Despoine, for example, was decorated with dancing figures with animal heads in human garments, and the Artemis of this group held a torch in one hand and two serpents in the other. This depiction shows that these goddesses are akin to the "Mistress of Animals" and the Minoan goddess of nature.

This umbilical connection of Artemis and her predecessors survives well past the Hellenistic period and into the development of early Christianity. Walbank confirms this in his analysis of a late Palestinian inscription (*SEG* 16.787) that gives Artemis the

---

[57] Nilsson 1971, *Minoan-Mycenaean Religion,* p. 504.

title *Despoine*.[58] Consequently, there can be little doubt that the epithet of "Mistress" was popularly applied to Artemis as part of what Nilsson describes as the introduction of an indigenous deity into the Greek pantheon.[59] He asserts that the Greeks purposely maintained several religions of indigenous origin while assimilating divinities into their own religious structure.

It is logical that Artemis evolved into the realm of the afterlife. One of the most significant aspects in making this connection is her title as "Mistress." This is especially important because it is easy to trace the repeated inheritance of this title in the worship of Artemis. Artemis evolves over time and space from the Egyptian goddess Neith, referred to as the "Mistress of the Bow and Ruler of the Arrows," to the Minoan "Mistress of Animals," and eventually to the Greek "Mistress of the Hunt." Although there is some controversy about whether other goddesses of the Greek pantheon, such as Hera and Athena, are also referred to as "Mistress,"[60] it is popularly agreed among scholars that Artemis is the only goddess to whom the title *Despoine* applies prolifically. As a result, it is not a surprise that she, not Hera or Athena, stands inside the temples of mystery cults and guards the door to the afterlife.

In the next chapter, the worship of Greek Artemis and the continuous evolution of her divine characteristics will be examined. Several of her roles will be highlighted, particularly

---

[58] Walbank 1981, p. 79. According to Walbank, the title *Despoine* is a very late inscription from Palestine. Walbank claims that an earlier version of the inscription from the Classical period does not use this title in reference to Artemis. However, he acknowledges that during the Palestinian period an addition was made to her titles and *Despoine* is a definite reference to Artemis. It is significant that in the later period Artemis is considered *Despoine*.

[59] Nilsson 1971, *Minoan-Mycenaean Religion,* p. 2.

[60] Walbank 1986, p. 280.

her role as "Saviour" and as "Patroness of Initiation," as well as her blood thirst, which often places her in the trifecta position of judge, jury, and executioner. As we have already seen, all these attributes have evolved from her pre-Greek status, but it is important to understand not only her significant position as a goddess of antiquity, but also the magnitude of her influence on the Greek community of her worshippers.

Thus, we see that Artemis transformed the ancient world by unifying many disparate practices across many goddess cults in a wide variety of regions, and by providing comfort to millions as they experienced different stages in life: birth, adulthood, marriage, old age, and death. She was the goddess for all generations, for all cultures, and in many ways her worship allowed for spiritual connections through a deep and instinctive understanding of nature and its transformative experience. She was as ever-changing and as adaptive as the seasons, and as a result, her worship survived all cultural conquests and varying ritual interpretations.

Hymn to Artemis

... beginning with the time when sitting on her father's knees — still a little maid — she spoke these words to her sire [Zeus]:

"Give me to keep my maidenhood, Father, forever:
and give me to be of many names,
that Phoebus [Apollo] may not vie with me.
And give me arrows and a bow,
give me to be Bringer of Light,
and give me to gird a tunic with embroidered border
reaching to the knee,
that I may slay wild beasts.
And give me sixty daughters of Oceanus for my choir —
all nine years old, all maidens yet ungirdled;
and give me for handmaidens twenty nymphs of Amnisus
who shall tend well my buskins, and, when I shoot no
more at lynx or stag,
shall tend my swift hounds.
And give to me all mountains;
and for city, assign me any, even whatsoever thou wilt."

And her father smiled and bowed assent.

—Callimachus, *Hymn* 3.1–28[61]

---

[61] Callimachus., and Robert Allason Furness. *Poems Of Callimachus.* J. Cape, 1931.

CHAPTER THREE

The Embodiment of Duality: Representations of Artemis in Greek Ritual

Sôteira: Artemis as Saviour

One of the fundamental roles that Artemis plays in Greek ritual is as *Sôteira*, "Saviour." Under this title, Artemis is worshiped for a variety of saving deeds. It is, for example, as the *Sôteira* who heals that she cures Eurypylus of his madness, and in gratitude he builds a temple in her honour (Pausanias 7.19.1–20.1). Her temple in Megara also stands in honour of *Sôteira*, built as an offering for her assistance to the Megarians in battle (Pausanias 1.40.2). According to legend, it is under this title as "Saviour" that she even assists Theseus in defeating the Minotaur. Pausanias states,

> In the marketplace of Troezen is a temple of Artemis *Sôteira*, with images of the goddess. It was said that the temple was founded, and

the name "Saviour" given by Theseus when he
returned from Crete after overcoming Asterion,
the son of Minos. This victory he considered the
most noteworthy of his achievements, not so
much, in my opinion, because Asterion was the
bravest of those killed by Theseus, but because
his success in unravelling the difficult Maze and
in escaping unnoticed after the exploit made
credible the saying that it was divine providence
that brought Theseus and his company back in
safety. (Pausanias 2.31.1)

Additionally, Artemis *Sôteira* is also worshipped by surviving
Trojans, who settled in the city of Boeae and built their city
around the sacred site of the myrtle tree (Pausanias 3.22.2).
Artemis' role as "Saviour" differs from the Christian conception
of salvation, however, which focuses on eternal life and
redemption from death. Nonetheless, as the goddess who
provides for a pain-free or less painful transition from life into
death, Artemis *Sôteira* plays a significant role in the performance
of last rites for her worshipers.

When Odysseus encounters the ghost of his mother Anticlea
in the underworld, he asks her if she died of illness or by the
arrows of Artemis (Homer, *Odyssey* 11.163). Homer also tells
of an island called Syria, above Ortygia, where the sun always
shines and there is good land and no one grows old or has any
sickness because Apollo of the silver bow comes with Artemis,
and they use their gentle arrows to give all the citizens of this
island an easy and peaceful death (*Odyssey* 15.403). Artemis is
often at the centre of stories about painless death, and many of
her followers pray to her for a merciful sleep. In the latter half
of the *Odyssey*, Penelope wishes that Artemis would give her the

peace of death and pierce her heart with a golden arrow and ease her pain (18.202, 20.061). There is something powerful in the position of Artemis as "Saviour." Here, she is not just protectress or mother, as Artemis Eileithyia, but straddles the boundaries between life and death. She is the merciful killer. This duality between the active healing, which gives life, and the active slaying, which takes life, is what makes Artemis singularly important within the Greek pantheon.

Callimachus refers to Artemis as "Queen" and asserts that when Artemis was a young girl sitting on her father Zeus' knees, asking him to allow her to keep her maidenhood forever and receive her bow and arrows, she also asked him to be *Phosphorus*, or "Bringer of Light," which became one of her many titles (Callimachus, *Hymn* 3.1). One of her most popular temples as "Bringer of Light" is at Messene in the sanctuary of Asclepius (Pausanias 4.31.10). Zeus is more than delighted to give her all that she asks for: "three times ten cities and towers more than one live vouchsafe thee — three times ten cities that shall not note to glorify any other god but to glorify the only and be called of Artemis. And thou shall be Watcher over Streets and Harbors" (Callimachus, *Hymn* 3.28). Thus, in addition to her being *Phosphorus*, she is also *Enodia*, "Protector of the Mariners." Consequently, Artemis is not only "Saviour" through mercy — that is, people do not only pray to her for protection and peaceful death — but she is "Saviour" in a way that is omnipresent. As the "Bringer of Light," her luminance literally saves ships, harbors, and all those who depend on these facilities to survive.

In her role as *Sôteira*, Artemis inhabits the personal spaces of her community of worshipers. As a goddess of mercy, she is invoked as *Phôsphoros*, meaning "Bringer of Light," and she is often *Hêmerasia*. or "She Who Soothes." Nilsson argues that these are positive and nurturing attributes that were granted to her in the Classical period.[62] While this may be true, it is significant that her ritual worship expanded from "Huntress," or goddess of wilderness, to the "Saviour" of her supplicants and the "Protector" of communities and cities. I argue that these two attributes make her the most significant Olympian goddess.

Artemis Strangled: The Patron of Initiation

Apankhomene, the strangled goddess, is another surname of Artemis. Tradition claims that in the neighborhood of the town of Caphyae in Arcadia, in a place called Condylea, there was a sacred grove of Artemis Condyleatis. Some children had playfully tied a rope around the neck of her statue and claimed she was strangled. As a result, the children were stoned to death by the villagers. Sometime later, the women of Caphyae were struck with a disease and all their children were stillborn. The villagers saw this as a sign of the wrath of Artemis for stoning the children, and the Oracle ordered that the children be buried properly and that annual sacrifices be made to them since they were wrongly killed. From then on, Artemis was called *Apankhomene*, or "Strangled" (Pausanias 8.23.6–7). This legend embodies the role of the goddess in children's lives. In her position as *Kourotrophos*, meaning "bringing up boys" or "rearing boys," she protects their upbringing and leads them to adulthood, receiving dedications of children's toys and garments.

It is important that in this legend we see that the children are correct to call Artemis "Strangled," as this title reveals a more ancient truth. The earliest use of the term *Apankhomene*

---

[62] Nilsson 1971, *Minoan-Mycenaean Religion*, p. 503.

arises from the image of hanging vegetation deities on trees.[63] This traces her roots back to the Minoan period, before Artemis was attached to her name. King argues that strangulation for the Greeks meant giving no blood. In the field of sacrifice, the shedding of blood issues a communication between men and the gods (Herodotus, *Histories* 4.60). However, as a form of human death, strangulation or hanging evoked horror (see, for example, Phaedra in Euripides, *Hippolytus* 778 and 802). As a form of suicide, strangulation and the option to give no blood in the face of violence such as rape or unwanted defloration was traditionally appropriate.[64] As eternal *Parthenos* ("Maiden"), Artemis does not shed her blood in the hunt, in sex, or in childbirth. Fundamentally, the duality of Artemis strangled is primarily evident in the fact that she is a goddess who does not bleed, but who makes others bleed.

King posits that Artemis being strangled, and therefore without blood, allows her to lead in the transition of *parthenoi* ("maidens") into *gynes* ("women") by initiating them into this new phase of life, which is identified with menstruation, marriage, and childbirth. Artemis is both bound and can release, and her duality in this ritual, and her position as a transitory agent between child and woman, or child and man, is fundamental. On the one hand, Artemis is thus *Lysizonos*, "Releaser of the Girdle."[65] She is powerful in the lives of women and often invoked as *Lysizonos* by women during childbirth, after which their girdles are dedicated to her.[66] King notes that also dedicated to Artemis is the *lochia*, the placenta, which can

---

[63] Farnell 1977, p. 428.

[64] King 1993, p. 119.

[65] In the Greek tradition, the girdle is put on at puberty and later dedicated to Artemis as a part of the marriage process. A special girdle is worn on the wedding night, and a woman unties her girdle to give birth.

[66] King 1993, p. 121.

likewise be invoked as a name for the goddess.[67] This clearly depicts her responsibility as overseer of the transition of females from *parthenoi* into *gynes*.

On the other hand, Artemis stands as *Philomeirax*, "Protector" of young girls, whose successful conversion from virgin maidens to effective procreators is solely her domain. Pausanias refers to her as *Lygodesma*, meaning bound with the plant called *lygos* or *agnos castus*. This epithet is an alternative title to Artemis *Orthia*, and it is explained by the account in which this cult image was found in a thicket of the *agnos* plant, which made it stand upright (*orthos*) (Pausanias 3.16.11). Claude Calame has isolated several possible connections between Artemis and the *lygos/agnos* plant.[68] He states that in the ancient world, the plant was used in wicker work and perfume-making, in medicines, and for a number of ritual purposes. The *lygos/agnos* plant has flexibility, as it can be made into rope that can bind, and its medical qualities encourage menstruation and lactation.[69] The analogy between Artemis straddling both the very early stages of life and women's reproductive stages is further evidenced when we consider that Artemis, as strangled, is bound with the *lygos*, and that she is also "Releaser of the Girdle," leading young girls through their first menstruation, which is induced by *agnos* when ingested. Thus, she spans the two temporal aspects of "woman": strangled, non-bleeding *parthenos* and released, bleeding *gyne*.[70] Yet, though she is concerned with the evolution from one period of life to another, she herself stays firmly on one side. She remains in the position

[67] Ibid., p. 121.
[68] Calame 1997, pp. 285–289.
[69] Ibid., p. 288.
[70] King 1993, p. 123.

of *Parthenos* while dictating and assisting in the development and success of *gynes*.

Thus, Artemis *Apankhomene* is another example of how the goddess encompasses all aspects of life, despite their seemingly opposite elements. By clinging to her ancient roots, she maintains the wilderness, the violence, and the freedom of being a nature goddess. At the same time, in wearing the mantle of her responsibility in Greek ritual she exhibits the qualities of nurse, saviour, and mother. These attributes can be clearly seen as she is revered both as a protector and a terrifying enforcer. Artemis is the embodiment of opposites, duality, and the paradox of protection and punishment. Like many of her predecessors, from whom she inherits all responsibilities, she is a goddess of totality. As the goddess in charge of the sum of all aspects of Greek life, it is only logical that Artemis not only preside over rituals that involve healing, birth, marriage, and other life-giving rituals, but that she also oversee rites that involve aspects of war, sacrifice, and blood. This supports the argument that Artemis is a goddess of transition and life passages, playing a fundamental role in the community of her followers at all stages in their lives.

The Bear of Brauron and Artemis Orthia: Blood Thirst and Sacrifice

The cult of Artemis *Brauronia* had two sanctuaries: one at the ancient site of Brauron (from which the goddess derives her name), and the other in the heart of Athens on the Acropolis. Pisistratus, the sixth-century BCE tyrant of Athens, was originally from Brauron and is credited with setting up the sanctuary of Artemis *Brauronia* on the Acropolis and thereby changing this community from a local to a state cult. After that, a procession was held every four years — from the Temple of Artemis *Brauronia* on the Athenian Acropolis to Brauron — in honour of the goddess and her priestess Iphigenia. Initially, it is easy to identify one aspect of Artemis' duality here when considering that this procession encompasses two different urban spaces, the city and the village. In addition to this, the rituals that took place at Brauron provide us with a much more complex identity for Artemis.

The sanctuary of Brauron was excavated by John Papadimitriou in 1948. Unfortunately, he died suddenly in 1963 and the results of the excavation project took another forty years to be made public. While many of the archeological findings have now been catalogued, it appears that only a small sample of the "hundreds and hundreds of *krateriskoi* found all over the sanctuary" at Brauron have been published.[71] Artemis of Brauron, also known as the Taurian Artemis, is mystical, and her worship was orgiastic and connected, at least in early times, with human sacrifice. According to Greek legend, there was in Tauris a goddess, whom the Greeks identified with their own Artemis, to whom all strangers that were thrown off the coast of Tauris were sacrificed (Euripides, *Iphigenia in Tauris* 36). It is this worship at Brauron that exposes the significance of Artemis in Greek life.

The rituals at Brauron are said to be initiation rituals for young girls that were thought of as *arktoi* — "she bears." It is important to note that the testimonium on which interpretations of these rituals were made is mostly dependent on the passage in Aristophanes' *Lysistrata* in which the chorus describes the various ritual functions they undertook: "*arrephoros* at seven, miller for *Archegetis* at ten, then wearing [or shedding] the *krokotos*, I was bear at the Brauronia, and then being a pretty girl, I was

---

[71] Moon 1983, p. 235.

kanephoros wearing a fig necklace" (Aristophanes, *Lysistrata* 641–646).[72] The life cycle of bears and their behaviours and similarities with man were studied in ancient times by Aristotle, Theophrastus, and Pliny. However, archaeological evidence for the image of a bear as mother goes back to the Neolithic period. This Neolithic image portrays the "notable tenderness of the mother beast for her cub as an image for human mothering."[73] Baring and Cashford suggest that the bear is "probably the oldest sacred animal of all."[74] These images are linked to the Brauron initiations into womanhood and motherhood, as well as the suggestion that Artemis is a derivative of an ancient bear goddess. The authors note that the bear is "the oldest animal hunted for food in the northern hemisphere, and also the oldest animal whose remains have been given a ritual significance."[75] This complex imagery of the bear as caregiver, but also as a large violent animal, is in many ways an anthropomorphic representation of the goddess herself. Under her care, young women are protected in the transition from child to adult; however, there is also an animalistic character to this ritual. In order to be transformed from girl to woman, the young girl must shed the uninhibitedness of her childhood and offer it as sacrifice to Artemis.

This is a ritual of "wildness." When girls who were coming of age were seen as being especially hormonal, they were said to be in the grip of the wild, independent goddess herself. By performing these rituals, it was believed that the goddess would guide the girls to maturity. Walbank agrees that the *arktoi* were prepubescent girls who shed their saffron robes as an initiation

---

[72] Hamilton 1989, p. 460.
[73] Baring and Cashford 1991, p. 71.
[74] Ibid., p. 28.
[75] Ibid., p. 29.

rite at the age of ten.[76] As evidence, he refers to an inscription that reads, "Then I was a miller of corn; and when I was ten years old I let drop for the *Archegetis* [Artemis] my yellow robe as a bear at the Brauronia."[77] These robes were then dedicated to Artemis.

Before marriage, every Athenian girl had to sacrifice *protelia* ("offerings") to Artemis. Childish things would be dedicated to the goddess as the girls were seen to be leaving their prepubescent "wildness" behind and entering womanhood and marriage (the realm of the goddess Hera). It is for *protelia* that Lloyd Jones argues that Iphigenia was brought to Aulis.[78] The first appearance of Iphigenia as the daughter of Agamemnon is in the *Cypria* fragment. Here, Stasinus of Cyprus describes how Iphigenia was brought to her father under the guise of marrying Achilles (*Cypria* frag. 1). While Hesiod states that Iphigenia was not killed but rather turned into Hecate and made a handmaid of Artemis (*Catalogue of Women* frag. 71; see also Pausanias 1.43.1), in the *Cypria* fragment, she is carried off to Tauris and made into a goddess by Artemis. In *Metamorphoses*, Antoninus Liberalis describes the event as follows:

> Artemis made a bull calf appear by the altar instead of Iphigenia whom she carried off far away from Greece, to the Sea of Pontus with its welcoming name of Euxinos, to Thoas son of Borysthenes [the Dnieper River]. She called the tribe of nomads there Taurians because a bull [*tauros*] had appeared instead of Iphigenia

---

[76] Walbank 1986, p. 276.
[77] Ibid., p. 277.
[78] Lloyd Jones 1983, p. 91.

on the altar. She also named her Tauropolos.
(Antoninus Liberalis, *Metamorphoses* 27)

It has long been conjectured that Iphigenia was originally a Minoan goddess and later subordinated to Artemis.[79] In fact, it is believed that Iphigenia and Orestes brought the image of Artemis from Tauris and landed at Brauron in Attica, where the goddess derived the name of Artemis *Brauronia* (Pausanias 1.23.9, 1.33.1). This wooden image, we are told by Pausanias, was carried away by Xerxes, King of Persia, who looted Athens and the nearby regions after his initial victory over the Greeks (Pausanias 8.46.3). It is also at Brauron that Iphigenia is said to have died and been buried. The myths surrounding Artemis *Brauronia*, particularly in regard to Iphigenia, reveal an intriguing aspect of the duality of Artemis at this location. Although the ritual offering of the *protelia* appears to be a practice centred on the lives of young girls as they transition from prepuberty to adulthood, the association between the goddess and the very masculine image of a bull requires a more complicated analysis of both this ritual and the myths that inspire it. Further examination will reveal that the rituals performed at Brauron, as well as the Spartan rite of sacrifice for Artemis *Orthia*, represent relics of an ancient past that were transfigured by the moralities of the Hellenistic period.

The Brauronian Artemis was also worshipped in Sparta as Artemis *Orthia*, goddess of the steep, or "she who stands erect." The latter, sometimes understood as a phallic symbol, may correlate with the fact that only boys participated in this ritual. Her image is said to have been brought over, or stolen, from Brauron and consequently drove men mad.[80] Tradition states

---

[79] Farnell 1977, p. 55.
[80] Redfield 1990, p. 128.

that some quarrel or competition among the earliest tribes of Sparta led to violence and death around the altar of Artemis. After the slaughter there was a plague, and the Oracle prescribed that the altar be soaked in blood. The citizens selected an individual by lot who would be the human sacrifice (Herodotus, *Histories* 1.65). This original tradition was eventually considered barbaric, and the ritual was adapted by the legendary lawgiver Lycurgus so that boys were scourged at her altar in such a manner that it became sprinkled with their blood. This cruel ceremony was believed to have been introduced in the place of human sacrifices,[81] and according to Redfield, it was not boys who were scourged but warriors, and instead of one of them dying they could all bleed together.[82] This is a very Spartan ritual in that it involves physical sacrifice in the sacred place of the divine. More interestingly, the ritual of the community is inscribed on the body of its citizens and denies differences, both natural and cultural, so that all men are treated equally.[83] Since this is clearly an initiation rite, we can see that Artemis is present in the transformation from child to adult of not just women but men too. This is further evidenced when we look at the tradition of the Taurian Artemis.

Orestes is said to have continued on from Brauron and established the cult of Artemis *Tauropolos*. A kindred divinity, if not the same as the Taurian Artemis, her worship was connected with bloody sacrifices, and she is said to have produced madness

---

[81] Nicholson, Oliver. *The Oxford Dictionary Of Late Antiquity.* Oxford University Press, 2018.

[82] Redfield 1990, p. 128.

[83] Ibid., p. 129. Redfield claims that the demand of the god is equality, and thus the function of the divine within Spartan ritual is to make sure this equality is maintained. Artemis is the embodiment of this sentiment as she presides over both male and female initiation rites in which participation is both necessary and equal.

in the minds of men if they looked upon her statue (Sophocles, *Ajax* 172). Artemis was able to cure this madness in her role as "Healer," but she did this sparingly and only for those she deemed worthy of her gift. According to Sophocles, Artemis *Tauropolos* was originally a designation of an ancient Taurian goddess who oversaw male rites of passage. The name *Tauropolos* has been explained in different ways, some supposing that it means the goddess worshipped in Tauris, who protects the country of Tauris, and to whom bulls are sacrificed (Sophocles, *Ajax* 172), while others explain it to mean the goddess riding on bulls, drawn by bulls, or killing bulls (Euripides, *Iphigenia in Tauris* 1457). Both explanations seem to have one thing in common, namely, that the bull was probably the ancient symbol of the bloody and savage worship of the Taurian divinity. The bull is mostly referred to by classics scholars as an ancient and proliferous symbol of masculinity. It is thus intriguing that Artemis is associated with this symbol, though not altogether surprising when we consider her duality as a goddess of bloodshed and retribution, often viewed as Greek male characteristics, as well as mercy and healing, often viewed as Greek female responsibilities. This shows the complexity of cultic practice, which places Artemis in the position of presiding divinity in the early lives of Greek boys and girls.

Festivals of Cakes, Fire, and Human Sacrifice

The ancient Greeks did not have one universally accepted calendar. Each city-state had its own, and they were often based on both the lunar and solar cycles. This makes it difficult to date, or time, the exact celebrations performed for Artemis throughout the year, but according to Sorita D'Este, "The Attic calendar which was used in Athens had two months in the spring which were named after Artemis *Elaphebolos* and Artemis *Mounykhia*."[84] This illustrates the importance of Artemis in the city of Athens. D'Este also claims that in Delos, the state calendar had one entire month named *Artemision* in honour of the goddess. But even when we do not know their exact dates, we know that numerous festivals and rites were held at many of Artemis' temples and sanctuaries across the Greek world throughout the year. Most of our knowledge about these festivals comes from the ancient Greek travel writer Pausanias, who often mentions in passing the numerous ways in which Artemis is celebrated, assuming his readers are already familiar with these ceremonies. There are several festivals for which we have very little data other than Pausanias' own experiences, which are very briefly outlined. For example, the ancient traveller tells us that annual festivals were held in Olympia to Artemis *Daphnaii* (Daphne) and Artemis *Elephiaia*. He also claims that there was a festival held for Artemis *Hymnia* outside of Orchomenus in Arcadia, where priests of Artemis lived ascetic lives of purity and chastity, abstaining from sex and bathing and never entering private houses.[85]

D'Este has collected numerous festivals of Artemis, many of them mentioned by ancient authors as unintentional backdrops in the stories of battles or descriptions of celebrations. For example:

> A further festival is recorded by Xenophon, when he wrote of a failed attack on Thebes on the last day of a festival [to] Artemis *Eukleia*. The date for this event is given to be 392 BCE. Another festival is mentioned by Hesychius

---

[84] D'Este 2005, p. 28.
[85] Ibid., p. 29.

when he when he referred to female dancers
from Sparta who danced at a festival for Artemis
Korythalia.[86]

As a result, we can conclude that the details of many festivals
to Artemis have been lost simply because everyone in the
community understood the celebrations were in her honour.
Perhaps this is why classicists have overlooked her in favour of
more documented Olympians such as Athena and Dionysius.
Here, we will discuss in some detail the festivals that were widely
celebrated in honour of the goddess and confirmed by many
ancient scholars, including the detailed works of Pausanias and
Herodotus.

One of the more popular festivals to Artemis is the
Charisteria ("thanksgiving"), which took place on the sixth
day of *Boedromion* (September). According to Herodotus,
there was already a long-standing, ancient celebration on
this day for the goddess Artemis (and her brother Apollo),
however, at some later time, the festival was enlarged and
became associated with the Battle of Marathon. The Greeks
honoured their victory over the Persians by celebrating the
goddess who brought them victory, "and the figure of the
goddess eclipsed more or less completely the presence of her
brother the sun-god in the festival of the sixth."[87] Miltiades,
an Athenian warrior who is often credited with devising the
tactics that defeated the Persians at the Battle of Marathon,
is said to have been the first to offer sacrifice to Artemis on
the day of her ancient feast. Pausanias tells us that, as part
of this same festival, 500 goats were sacrificed to Artemis
Agrotera and Ares *Enyalios*. The goats were taken into the

---

[86] Ibid., p. 29.
[87] Macan 1895, p. 224.

temple on Ilissos in a ceremonial procession and sacrificed collectively. It was said that each goat was meant to represent a fallen Persian soldier, but that so many Persians had died in the battle that doing so would have culled the entire goat population.[88] What makes this festival especially interesting is that the sacrifices were offered at a temple of Artemis and Ares, which is a unique collaboration by these two divinities and speaks widely to their elated position in battle worship and war.

Another popular festival, that of *Elaphobolia*, takes place on the sixth day of Elaphebolion (March/April) and may have been named after the *elaphos* cakes in the story of the Samian rescue of 300 boys told by Herodotus (*Histories* 3.48). The Corinthians had captured 300 sons of noble Corcyraeans and were offering them as eunuchs in the city of Alyattes. When the men escorting the boys stopped in the city of Samos, the Samians were horrified to discover the purpose of their journey. In an attempt to save the boys from their fate, the Samians told the boys to hide in the sanctuary of the temple of Artemis. When the Corinthians heard where the boys were hiding, they knew they could not enter the sanctuary to retrieve them, so they blocked all food and supplies going to the sacred temple, intending to starve them out. In response, the Samians invented a festival, which they continued to perform well into Herodotus' lifetime:

> Each evening, as night closed in, during the whole time that the boys continued there, choirs of youths and virgins were placed about the temple, carrying in their hands cakes made of sesame and honey [*elaphos*] in order that

---

[88] Ibid., p. 30.

the Corcyraean boys might snatch the cakes
and so get enough to live upon. (Herodotus,
Histories 3.48)

This nightly dancing around the temple with cakes in hand
went on for so long that the Corinthians were forced to
give up their ownership of the boys and leave Samos. Once
the boys were free of their fate, the Samians returned them
to their home of Corcyra, but this festival of salvation and
ingenuity continued in honour of the goddess for generations
thereafter. Many other states besides Samos celebrated the
festival of *Elaphobolia*, but in many cases different stories
of origin were told and other events were also included in
the feasts and celebrations. For example, in the town of
Hyampolis, in Phocis, citizens similarly celebrate Artemis on
the sixth day of Elaphebolion, but the festival's origin story is
based on the victory of the townspeople over the Thessalians,
who had been ravaging the surrounding countryside. In
this case, *elaphos* cakes made of dough, honey, and sesame
seeds in the shape of deer are offered to Artemis *Elaphebolos*
during the festivities.[89] Whatever the source of the festival
may be, Artemis is central to the celebrations in the month
of Elaphebolion and honoured repeatedly as the saviour of
young men, as well as the protector of townspeople who offer
her piety and sweet sustenance.

The cult of Artemis *Laphria* was a somewhat more gruesome
ritual performed yearly in honour of the goddess. It is said by
Pausanias that the goddess was surnamed *Laphria* after a man
of Phocis, because the ancient image of Artemis was set up at
Calydon by Laphrius, the son of Castalius, son of Delphus. The
image represents her in the guise of a huntress, and it is made

---

[89] Parke 1994, p. 125-136.

of ivory and gold (Pausanias 7.18.9–10). Every year the people of Patrae celebrate this festival, where many different animals are burned alive:

> Round the altar in a circle, they set up logs of wood still green, each of them sixteen cubits long. On the altar within the circle is placed the driest of their wood. Just before the time of the festival they construct a smooth ascent to the altar, piling earth upon the altar steps.

> The festival begins with a most splendid procession in honour of Artemis, and the maiden officiating as priestess rides last in the procession upon a cart yoked to deer. It is, however, not till the next day that the sacrifice is offered, and the festival is not only a state function but also quite a popular general holiday. For the people throw alive upon the altar edible birds and every kind of victim as well; there are wild boars, deer and gazelles; some bring wolf-cubs or bear-cubs, others the full-grown beasts. They also place upon the altar fruit of cultivated trees.

> Next, they set fire to the wood. At this point I have seen some of the beasts, including a bear, forcing their way outside at the first rush of the flames, some of them actually escaping by their strength. But those who threw them in drag them back again to the pyre. It is not remembered that anybody has ever been wounded by the beasts. (Pausanias 7.18.11–13)

Although grim by modern standards, this was an especially important state festival, and the main festival days were public holidays that allowed all citizens to participate. Pausanias claims that no one wounded the beasts meant for sacrifice, which seems to him an important factor. While Artemis demanded the sacrifice of live animals, there seems to be a very clear emphasis that such an act should not be enjoyed in any sort of sadistic way by harming or torturing the animals offered in her honour.

Artemis Triklaria: The Trifecta of Judge, Jury, and Executioner

The cult of Artemis *Triklaria,* or "Unyielding," can be traced to the old town of Patras, while it was still an Ionian community. Pausanias tells us that they had a precinct and a temple in the goddess's honour where they used to celebrate every year with a festival and an all-night vigil (Pausanias 7.19.1). The priesthood of the goddess was held by a maiden until the time came for her to be married. Tradition states that at one time a particularly beautiful maiden named Comaitho had an equally beautiful lover named Melanippos. The couple wanted to get married but both their parents declined their request for a wedding. Overwhelmed by their desire for one another, they made love in the temple of the goddess (Pausanias 7.20.1). Artemis was angered by this transgression and "began to destroy the inhabitants; the earth yielded no harvest, and strange diseases occurred of an unusually fatal character" (Pausanias 7.20.5). The community sent for the Oracle at Delphi, and the Oracle named the guilty party and commanded that they be sacrificed to the goddess, and that afterward each year the most beautiful *pais* (young boy) and *parthenos* (maiden) should be sacrificed to ease Artemis' wrath. For this sacrifice, the river flowing past the sanctuary of Artemis *Triklaria* was called *Ameilikhos*, or "Relentless." Previously, the river had no name.

Pausanias tells us that this human sacrifice to Artemis came to an end when the Oracle claimed that a strange king would come to their land bringing a strange divinity (Pausanias 7.19.8). Legend claims that when the Greeks conquered Troy, and the spoils of war were divided, Eurypylus received a box containing the image of Dionysus, which when looked upon drove Eurypylus mad. In a moment of clarity, he inquired at the Oracle at Delphi about a solution for his crisis. The Oracle told him that he would come across a people offering a strange sacrifice and that there he should set down his box and make the place his home. Once he made port near Aroe, he witnessed the sacrifice of two young people for Artemis *Triklaria* and realized that this was the sacrifice the Oracle had predicted. While he realized he had found the place to call home, the people of Patras recognized him as the fulfillment of their own oracle and thus the ritual of human sacrifice was ended. The name of the river changed to *Meilikhos*, or "Yielding," and by the road that ran from the sea to the shore Eurypylus established a sanctuary and dedicated a stone statue to Artemis *Sôteira* in memory of his healing (Pausanias 7.18–21). It is significant that Artemis can be considered both "Unyielding," requiring human sacrifice, and "Saviour," healing the illnesses that befall her devotees. This points to the intrinsic position the worship of Artemis occupies in the lives of this community. That the goddess is "unyielding" and requires a bloody sacrifice as retribution is not surprising if we consider her Egyptian and Minoan ancestry. Here, we see that despite her role as merciful "Saviour," Artemis can also inspire fear, dread, and respect, which are characteristics of primeval matrifocal goddess traditions.

Thus, the duality and complexity of Artemis has been clearly evidenced. She is not a goddess whose worship is uniform, or who occupies a single theme, event, or lifecycle in Greek life. Her divinity is a combination and intersection of all aspects of human existence; from the beginning of life at birth through the innocence and wildness of childhood, Artemis guides the initiations and transitions of both boys and girls into adulthood, marriage, procreation, as well as through war, violence, and sacrifice. And when her devotees have reached the end of their existence, they pray to her so that she may gift them with a peaceful death. In addition, her worship involves all geographical spaces from the city to the village, to the sea, and to the mountains. As a result of her all-encompassing dominion over the lives of the Greeks, it is logical that Artemis may have also had a primary position in the rituals that involve the mysteries of the afterlife. The next and final chapter will discuss evidence that supports the view that Artemis was not only a goddess whose worship and traditions completely enveloped human life, but that she also had a fundamental role in Greek mystery religions whose details and practices remain largely obscure and unknown. Her association with the Egyptian Neith, and Bastet, possibly Hathor and even Isis,[90] as well as her inheritance from Minoan deities such as the "Mistress of Animals" and the goddess of nature, support the claim that she is very likely the mystery goddess known only as Despoine.

---

[90] Erman 1907, p. 13.

Cave Prayer to the Mother and the Womb

Root your feet into the ground,
feel the depth below you,
the strength of soil and earth,
that keeps you strong.

Open your heart to the womb of the earth,
the embrace of darkness,
the return to the mother.

You are where you are meant to be.
You have been returned to the womb,
you are waking,
and we are grateful.

Breathe in the strength of a millennia of prayer,
breathe out your fears and doubts.
Let the dark of the womb fill you with renewed faith and joy
feel the light in your chest,
the light that shines because darkness returned to you.

Be grateful for your breath,
your heart,
your body,
and the blood in your veins that sings at being one with the
womb again.

—C. Ionescu

CHAPTER FOUR

Lady of the Wild Things

It is easy to romanticize Artemis as the goddess of nature and wilderness — a maiden of the hunt. Many artists over the centuries have done exactly that, sculpting or painting her in the innocence of youth, frolicking through forests with her pretty nymphs and young deer. But we must remember that no matter how hard the Greeks tried to force her under their patriarchal parameters of femininity and childishness, she remained a wild entity, often unpredictable, vicious, and without remorse. As "Lady of the Wilderness," her association with animals is no surprise, but her connection to powerful beasts exemplifies the fierceness of her dominance and the reason why so many of her followers prayed for mercy and compassion.

As "Great Mother," the goddess nurtures and befriends all things being both animal and divine. Through her relationship with wild and often dangerous animals, she serves as a bridge linking humankind with the world of nature, for she transforms the fear we have of our animal drives and unites these untamed instincts with the expectations of our spiritual nature.[91] Getty

---

[91] Getty 1990, p. 78.

claims that "the divine feminine has always been linked with animals; from the insect world, as a bee, wasp or spider, to the domesticated cat, dog, horse and pig, onto the wild beasts of jungle and forest, and into the mythical realm of dragons and unicorns, the sphinx, sirens and mermaids."[92] As such, the mysteries of the environment have always resonated deeply with women and have connected them spiritually to a goddess that represents wilderness in the wild. This association between the wilderness of nature, the untamed being outside patriarchal society, or what male historians have labeled "civilized" society, was a key aspect of women's spiritual power. It was the mysteries of the mountains and forests, lakes and oceans, as well as the animals who lived free among them that allowed women to connect to the divine source of the goddess of the wilderness. As Pratt argues, "Women have always used nature to subvert culture, and the wild woman archetype has always appealed to us, as wild women are entirely outside the patrilineal and patriarchal system."[93] The Greek Artemis inherits a mantle of wilderness that is unlike any other deity in the Olympian pantheon. She is both huntress and protector, and her tools in myth and ritual are untamed beasts and sacred forests.

This archetype of the wild woman has been referred to by some scholars as "the Artemis archetype." The Artemis archetype is understood as a goddess of the wild who blends a healthy animality with a sense of balance of nature.[94] This archetype proves the connection between the Minoan and the Greek "Mistress of Animals." She is associated with the orgiastic dance and the sacred bow, both prominent features of the Minoan cult, and she is the mistress of water, nature, and

---

[92] Ibid., p. 80.
[93] Pratt 1999, p. 287.
[94] Ibid., p. 284.

of animals, which corresponds to the Minoan conception of the goddess of nature and animals depicted in surviving Minoan monuments. From this starting point, we may understand the two lines of development that lead, on the one hand, to the "Great Mountain Mother" of Asia Minor, who roams the mountains accompanied by her entourage, and on the other, to the virgin "Huntress" of Classical Greece. In the former, her archaic origins as a nature goddess, with representations of dying and reviving nature, and consequently the ecstatic and orgiastic elements of her cult, were emphasized. The latter development blended into Greek Olympian traditions, where she remained the "Mistress of Animals" and, because she was a sovereign goddess, did not tolerate any male partner; she became the severe virgin "Huntress" goddess. The popular conception of Artemis, which is much nearer to her origins, explains why the Greeks identified the Ephesian Artemis with their own Artemis. For the latter originates in the Minoan goddess of nature and animals and has kept much of her old character in the popular and rustic cult.[95]

Her unrestricted movement in nature, without the presence of males or a male protector, allows Artemis a type of freedom for which many women who live their daily lives under the rules and whims of men yearn. Even more enticing is her opposition to male companionship and marriage, but especially her ability to defend herself from being forced into a patriarchal union. Although the Greeks often tried to associate her worship and stories to her "twin" Apollo, Artemis' connection to nature, to the wild impulse of being 'like a deer' and running free, allows her to step outside the boundaries of gender expectations in a way that none of her fellow goddesses were able to do. While Athena is a

---

[95] Nilsson 1971, *Minoan-Mycenaean Religion*, p. 509.

virgin goddess of war and wisdom, she is often to be found in patriarchal spaces governed by law, and rules, and male-centred civic duty. Aphrodite is not a virgin, but she is trapped under the category of "love goddess," constantly chasing vanity, sexuality, and male consorts. Hera is forcibly married to a charlatan, while Demeter is shoved so deeply into a maternal role that she cannot think of anything else but her daughter Persephone for six months of the year. It is only Artemis, whether by coincidence or design, who remains free to wander through the forests, spend her time among nymphs and she-bears, and take her vengeance whenever and however she desires. She is untamed in a way that is not connected to her body or her chastity. She is untamed in the same way a wild animal is untamed, without responsibility or the constriction of divine duty. She moves according to her own whims and participates in mythic story on her own terms. This is evident when we consider the liberty of her priestesses: "The virginity of the priestesses who served her, and of the adolescent girls attending her shrine at Brauron, is that of women who retained the right to choose what to do with their bodies, whether to roam at will, or stay at home, whether to practice celibacy, or make love."[96] This autonomy afforded to women over their own bodies is revolutionary in a patriarchal system of control. One could argue that the priestesses of Artemis had more freedom over their own reproduction choices than women in many parts of the world have today. As Pomeroy points out, "either way as mother goddess or as virgin, Artemis retains control over herself; her lack of permanent connection to a male figure in a monogamous relationship is the keystone of her independence."[97]

---

[96] Pratt 1994, p. 291.
[97] Pomeroy 1995, p. 6.

Historically, scholars have treated wild women as slaves to rituals of untamed ecstasy and violence. Stories of the rituals of maenads in the cults of Dionysus, for example, have long been both exaggerated and exploited for voyeuristic consumption among male historians and myth writers. In this ecstatic ritual, which involved women dancing naked in the woods while wearing frightening masks depicting animals or gorgons, the god Dionysus himself is torn apart by his female followers drunk on wine and other hallucinogens. Through this act of dance and drink and song, the ecstasy of the wilderness and nature is experienced in its more orgiastic form. According to ancient historians and playwrights such as Herodotus and Aeschylus, this and similar rituals are not for the faint of heart, and their practice have deep connections to pre-Greek rituals of celebration and offerings that benefit the entire community. Yet this type of female drunkenness and aggression was both feared and frowned upon, despite the fact that the death and rebirth of the androgynous Dionysus was a mandatory act in an agricultural society that largely depended on the benevolence of a resurrected god. While Dionysus and Artemis are gods of the wild and closely linked both in worship and ritual, the type of wild experience and liberties Artemis offers her followers is less about mind-altering substances and the drunken ecstasy of maenads, and more about the use of nature as a tool through which choice over body and civic duty can be made with a clear mind and the secure knowledge that whatever choice is made by her supplicants is under the full protection of a fearsome divinity. Artemis fearlessly defends the choices of her followers in the sacred space she creates in the forests and mountains over which she rules. As Pratt writes, "The wild women inhabit a free zone closely impinging upon culture, a zone of partially repressed paganism which can easily rupture the patriarchal pie. The urge to marry or join the wild women in the woods is constant in European folklore, where escaping culture for the wildwood and patriarchal matrimony for Diana [Artemis] is as likely to lead to empowerment as death."[98]

Lions and Deer and Bears, Oh My!

Minoan frescoes and seals of the sixteenth century BCE reveal that Artemis is not only a goddess of childbirth, but that she is also the incarnation of the fertility of nature. She is the "Queen of the Mountains" portrayed standing on the mountain top, and she is the "Mistress of Animals" shown flanked by dogs or lions.[99] The "Lady of the Wild Things" is a complex embodiment of mercy and aggression, life and death, the natural and the supernatural. Her realm in the wilderness is her seat of power because it stands outside the very structure that claims to have monopoly over power: the patriarchal world. So often, in modern depictions of wealth and success, we think of money and careers. That is because humans all over the world have accepted the notion that the "new world" is a progression from an "old world." The masculine, or cerebral, perception is that time moves in a straight line, and that on the modern side of this line is "progress." As such, many of us have lost contact with, or simply have never known, the raw power of goddess worship, in particular, wild goddess worship. Artemis has stood in the wild forests, dancing in the moonlight and leading the pack for thousands of years. For centuries, scholars have tried to label her as young, virginal, irrelevant. But despite this dismissal, she has survived the onslaught of new religions, the exaggerated popularity of her fellow female Olympians, and

---

[98] Pratt 1994, p. 286.
[99] Gimbutas 1991, p. 109.

the continuous destruction of her sacred realm. She has survived as nature has survived. Her bears, lions, deer, and other animals have struggled to outlast the onslaught of this so-called man-made progress, and there is hope that women will once again turn to her for wisdom, strength, and protection.

The Bear Mother

Not many people think of Greece when they imagine a thriving bear habitat. Most of us think of places like the Rocky Mountains in Canada, or the deep and dangerous Scandinavian forests, where grizzly bears, brown bears, or black bears run free. However, brown bears have long made a home in Northern Greece, particularly the Pindus Mountains, for thousands of years. Much of Greek mythology, particularly the worship of Artemis, revolved around the beauty and majesty of brown bears and their dominance over the indigenous animal ecosystem of this part of the Mediterranean. Today, an NGO aptly named Callisto is in charge of the 450 to 700 remaining bears known to roam across the Rhodopes Mountains, which border Bulgaria, and the Pindus mountain range, bordering southern Albania. In the ancient world of the Greeks, this area had a flourishing bear population that has now dwindled due to poaching and loss of habitat. NGOs such as Callisto work with the communities and villages in these mountains, as well as ecotourist groups, to maintain a safe space for the remaining bear families that make Northern Greece their home. According to Gimbutas, "The holiness of the bear, an animal of great strength and majesty, the glory of the forest, is universal in the northern hemisphere."[100] Folk memories across Northern Europe are full of stories that

---

[100] Ibid., p. 116.

worshipped the bear as an ancestor and a mother/life-giver. Gimbutas's work reveals linguistic evidence that associates the veneration of bears with pregnancy and birth: the old European root *bher* and Germanic *beran*, "to bear children," "to carry"; the Germanic *barnam*, "child"; the Old Norse *burdh*, "birth."[101] These root terminologies are evidence that the concept of bear as "mother" or "birthing" has archaic roots in many parts of Europe and, as such, is naturally associated with Artemis, especially under her mantle of protectress of childbirth, and of course in her role as "Mistress of Animals."

Throughout most of Europe, a plethora of ritual and practice has been built around "bear culture." For example, among the Belarussians it was believed that the appearance of a bear brought good luck to the village, and locals used to lead bears throughout their villages to make sure everyone received their blessings. In some villages in Bulgaria, there are stories that a bear was led into locals' homes and seated in honourable places near altars where icons of the goddess were hung. Some Slavic stories claim that the bear has healing powers, and sometimes if a person was sick, they would lie on the ground and allow a bear to walk over them in order to be healed.[102] Bears have long had a history of healing and benevolence within human communities, and we find their influence on divine ritual throughout the Mediterranean. Even today, according to Thompson, "in The Cave of Akrotiri, near ancient Cydonia in western Crete, a festival in honour of *Panagia Arkoudiotissa*, "Virgin Mary of the Bear," is celebrated on the second day of February."[103] It is interesting to see the connection between the Virgin Mary and the Virgin Artemis under the mantle of bear worship,

---

[101] Ibid., p. 116.

[102] Ibid., p. 118.

[103] Thompson 1962, p. 93 (see Gimbutas 1991, p. 116).

the difference between these two divine feminine characters being that Mary carries and births a son, while Artemis is forever the midwife of childbirth (according to Greek myth). Further evidence of bear divinities can also be found in the surviving Paleolothic "Bear Madonnas," Vinča figurines from the fifth millennium BCE in the form of a woman wearing a bear mask and holding a cub, and in another part of Europe, *Dea Artio*, the "Bear Goddess," is known to have been venerated by the Celts.[104] Thus, the bear is deeply entrenched in ritual and belief as a mother figure, a powerful symbol of both creation and protection, as well as of the dangerous physical burden of carrying and nourishing unborn life, which seem to reflect the physical strength and prowess of a mother bear.

As we saw in chapter 3, Artemis and her companions sometimes assumed the shape of bears, and Athenian girls danced as bears in honour of Artemis at Brauron. The term *arkteusai* means "to be a bear," and becoming a bear was often used in reference to the consecration of virgins to Artemis, before they were married off.[105] During rites of initiation, young girls become the bears of Artemis. One example is the archeological find at Sparta, where an interesting lead figure from the sanctuary of Artemis shows a female dancer wearing a bear mask.[106] The ancient Greeks saw bears everywhere, especially in the stars, and attributed the characteristics of the mother bear to Artemis, both as the creature and as the stellar constellation of Ursa Major, "the Great Bear."

Killing her sacred bears was the most certain way of bringing down Artemis' wrath, as the Athenians found out the hard way. Legend claims that a female bear once appeared in

---

[104] Gimbutas 1991, p. 116.
[105] D'Este 2005, p. 71.
[106] Gimbutas 1991, p. 116.

the shrine of Artemis at Mounykhia in Attica and was killed by the Athenians. Following the destruction of the bear, a famine ensued, which was seen by many as punishment for slaying Artemis' sacred bear:

> [Piraeus] was previously an island. This, in fact, is how it got its name: from the crossing [*diaperan*]. Mounykhos, who possessed its headlands, established a shrine of Artemis *Mounykhia*. After a female bear appeared in it and was done away with by the Athenians a famine ensued, and the god prophesied the means of relieving the famine: someone had to sacrifice his daughter to the goddess. Baros was the only one who undertook to do so, on the grounds that his family held the priesthood for life. He had his daughter adorned but then hid her in the same [shrine?] and dressed a goat up in her clothing and sacrificed it as though it were his daughter. (*Suidas* s.v. "Embaros") [107]

This was not the first time that Artemis became enraged by the destructions of wild things under her care. She is ferocious in her protection and possessiveness of the beasts she views as her own, and there are many stories that link the killing of one of her animals with severe and swift punishment. Killing a bear was seen as a direct act of violence and disrespect towards the "Lady of the Wild Things," and the Athenians, as well as other villagers living in the Mediterranean, learned quickly that her retribution as strict and unforgiving.

---

[107] SUIDAS. The Suda. Translation by various (Senior editor Whitehead, D.). The Suda On-Line http://www.stoa.org/sol/

Even more interesting than her swift vengeance for killing one of her animals was how Artemis used the wild as punishment for those who betrayed her sacred trust. It is somewhat ironic that the NGO in the Pindus Mountains is named Callisto, as this name is in honour of the well-known story of a young girl who fell from grace and was turned into a bear, which is more of a warning against violating the goddess's trust than a celebration of bear imagery. There are two versions of the myth of Callisto, both equally terrifying for anyone who makes the mistake of imagining Artemis as a childish maiden roaming innocently through the forests. Hesiod tells us that Callisto was initially a member of Artemis' entourage, joining the goddess in the forest and occupying herself with wild beasts in the mountains. Predictably, Zeus seduced the young girl behind Artemis' back and she became pregnant. When Artemis learned of the pregnancy, she was so enraged by the betrayal that she turned Callisto into a bear. Zeus, who (supposedly) felt sorry for his young lover's fate, took pity on her and turned her into the constellation Ursa Major:

> [Callisto] was the daughter of Lycaon and lived in Arcadia. She chose to occupy herself with wild beasts in the mountains together with Artemis, and, when she was seduced by Zeus, continued some time undetected by the goddess, but afterwards, when she was already with child, was seen by her bathing and so discovered. Upon this, the goddess was enraged and changed her into a beast. Thus, she became a bear and gave birth to a son called Arcas … but [later] Zeus delivered her because of her connection with him and put her among the stars, giving her the name "Bear" (*Arktos*)

because of the misfortune which had befallen her. (Hesiod, *Astronomy* frag. 3)

Hesiod's version of the story seems to favour Zeus and his inescapable charm and sympathy. It positions Artemis in the role of enraged and jealous "mother" or "sister" for the transgression of sex and pregnancy. It contradicts much of what we know about Artemis, particularly in her protection of mothers and children, and her work with pregnancy and childbirth. As such, Apollodorus' version of the same myth seems a better interpretation of Olympian behaviour and personalities:

> Eumelus [an eighth-century BCE poet] and certain others maintain that Lycaon had a daughter named Callisto, although Hesiod says she was one of the *Nymphai*, while Asios identifies her father as Nycteus, and Pherecydes as Ceteus. She was a hunting companion of Artemis, imitating her dress and remaining under oath a virgin for the goddess. But Zeus fell in love with her and forced her into bed, taking the likeness, some say, or Artemis, others, of Apollo. Because he wanted to escape the attention of Hera, Zeus changed Callisto into a bear. But Hera persuaded Artemis to shoot the girl with an arrow like a wild animal. There are those who maintain, however, that Artemis shot her because she did not protect her virginity. As Callisto died, Zeus seized his baby and handed it over to Maia to rear in Arcadia, giving it the name Arcas. Callisto he changed into a star, which he called *Arktos*. (Apollodorus, *Library* 3.100)

This version of the fate of Callisto is somewhat clearer; Zeus forcing himself on a young girl who had taken a vow of virginity (even if not interpreted in the physical/hymen sense) and turning her into a bear to hide her from Hera seems to be on trend with most stories of Zeus' forced "seductions." That being said, Hera convincing Artemis to shoot the woman-bear, the mother-bear, is hard to accept, but also in line with Artemis being a tool for Olympian vengeance and aiming her deathly arrows at humans who betray their vows to the gods (you may be shocked to learn the fate of Niobe and her children in the second part of this chapter). It is important to note that in Apollodorus' version, Zeus took on the likeness of either "Artemis or Apollo" in order to seduce Callisto. Callisto acquiescing to this seduction by either of the twins implies that there may be more to the relationship between Artemis and her maidens than platonic friendship. Furthermore, once Callisto became the constellation Ursa Major, her relationship with Artemis became even more intertwined as this star cluster continued to have a fundamental impact on the worship and ritual of the goddess, as well as her continued connection and association with the moon and the cosmos. The bear remains under the protection of the goddess to this day, and the fact that the NGO protecting brown bears in Northern Greece is named after this long-standing myth of Artemis and her Callisto speaks volumes for the continued influence of the wild goddess in her protection of the natural world and especially the habitat of one of her most favoured beasts.

The Lion among Women

The goddess of nature has a special relationship with the animal world. Various wild beasts and fantastic creatures such as griffins attend her or are nursed by her. A common type of representation is a seated goddess leading or petting a goat, a deer, or a lion.[108] Only the most powerful divinities are associated with felines. As we saw in chapter 1, the Egyptian goddesses Bastet and Sekhmet are feline divinities that inspire both awe and fear in their followers. One major difference between the Egyptian goddess compared to the Minoan "Lady of the Wild," however, is that the Minoan goddess is never depicted inside a shrine. She manifests within a natural environment and is often depicted as seated under a tree or on a rock. Another difference from Egyptian iconography is that the Minoan goddess is not attended by priests dressed in sacramental costume. Those that come close to her, either her animal servants or human worshipers, are mostly of the female sex.[109] As *Potnia Theron*, "Mistress of Animals" and "Lady of the Wild," Artemis is frequently depicted in association with lions and leopards.

Pausanias describes Artemis holding a lion in her left hand and a leopard in her right, which may correspond with depictions of *Potnia Theron* seen on several vases and pendants found across the Mediterranean that date as far back as to the seventh century BCE. Pausanias writes, "On what account Artemis has wings on her shoulders I do not know; in her right hand she grips a leopard, in her left a lion" (Pausanias 5.19.5). Two aspects of these depictions are interesting, one is the "winged" goddess, and the other is her hold on the beasts in question. The concept of winged divinities was a long-standing tradition during the Bronze Age when the bird goddess and the concept of flying, as a past times of gods, were embraced by many early Mediterranean civilizations. Nilsson, who contends that the "Mistress of Animals" was

---

[108] Marinatos 1993, p. 152.
[109] Ibid., p. 160.

often represented with wings, connects this material evidence to the winged depiction of Artemis and the "Mistress of Animals."[110] There have been several archeological finds where Artemis is depicted with hands spread out as long as wings, or with actual wings on her back. It is unclear whether or not it was an Olympian myth that literally "clipped her wings" to shape their maiden "Huntress" into the less imposing, less powerful maiden of the woods, or if Minoan traditions of the goddess of nature evolved away from winged divinities and the Olympic stories followed suit.

Felines, especially lions, have long been a symbol of power, strength, and royalty. Known colloquially as the "king of the jungle," this majestic characterization is often associated with male prowess and/or male dominance. Consequently, the connection between lion symbolism and female divinities gets lost among the numerous representations of European kings, who take on the mantle of this feline dominance. In fact, one of the most famous Disney movies, *The Lion King*, revolves around a father–son relationship, and the impact that dominant relationship has on the rest of the jungle. As a child, I found it fascinating that the "circle of life" theme, repeatedly celebrated throughout the film, centres on the image of a male adult (in this case a baboon/male shaman) holding up a male child as though this is the beginning and the end, the Alpha and Omega of life. Nowhere in the film is it acknowledged that procreation, or the actual "circle of life," begins and ends with female fecundity, pregnancy, and birth. Disney has a long tradition of misogynistic storytelling, but this brief example is evidence of not just a corporate patriarchal perspective, but the indoctrination of generations to believe that life is celebrated with the birth of a male heir.

---

[110] Nilsson 1971, *Minoan-Mycenaean Religion,* p. 506.

From a biological perspective, it is hard to deny the fact that male lions do very little as pack members other than protect the parameters of their territories. But anyone who has ever watched a nature documentary on lions and has sat through the awe and horror of a group of lionesses taking down a bull or antelope to feed their pack surely cannot help but be impressed by their physical strength and cunning in the hunt. As "Huntress," Artemis has more in common with the females of the "lion kingdom" than their lazier, less interesting male counterparts.

In the *Iliad*, Artemis is described as a lion among women, emphasizing her connection with felines, but even more importantly that her symbolic association with male lions is more about a royal, dominant connection than and biological reality: "Zeus has made you [Artemis] a lion among women, and given you leave to kill any at your pleasure" (Homer, *Iliad* 6.205). An abundant finding of royal and aristocratic seals at the palace of Knossos similarly shows the "Mistress of Animals" with lions at her side and a spear in her hand.[111] There are also several depictions of Artemis from the Greek Archaic period in which the goddess holds two lions by the neck with either of her hands, showing her control and power over these apex predators.[112] But most interesting of all are the depictions of her grabbing the lions by their hind legs (here the lions are hanging upside down), which shows her complete dominion over the "king of the jungle."[113]

In Aeschylus' play *Agamemnon*, Chalchis addresses Artemis as one who is gracious to the cubs of fierce lions (140–141),

[111] Nilsson 1971, *Minoan-Mycenaean Religion*, p. 366.

[112] *Artemis and the Big Cats.* Based on the image of Artemis Potnia on an eighth-century BCE vase found in Italy, this image shows the goddess holding a large feline in each hand. The image also clearly shows Artemis as a winged goddess; see D'Este 2005, p. 80.

[113] Nilsson 1971, *Minoan-Mycenaean Religion,* p. 506.

which could mean that the lion, and its fierceness, must have been regarded as an embodiment of this very quality in Artemis herself. For such reasons, lions (like deer) may sometimes have been kept in her sanctuaries. There is a suggestion of this custom in at least one of Theocritus' *Idylls*, where the visit to a grove of Artemis is described: "On that day, many wild beasts were paraded about the goddess in her honour, including a lioness" (Theocritus, *Idylls* 2.66–68). Elinor Bevan also refers to a fragment of the poet Alcman, quoted by Athenaeus, wherein a tame lioness is kept in the sanctuary of a deity. Athenaeus relates that during a night festival, "the making of a cheese from lion's milk took place."[114] It has been suggested by some that the unnamed deity is Dionysus, but Sam Wide believed (for grammatical reasons) that a female deity is to be understood, and that this deity was Artemis.[115] We have previously seen that the rituals and cultic traditions of Artemis and Dionysus often overlap, particularly around the concept of wilderness and the wild, and that the characteristics between practice and dance for the gods' celebrations are remarkably similar. The lion festival for Artemis would have been held in a Laconian sanctuary, but the sanctuary described by Theocritus was located in Sicily, and it was in Sicily, evidently, that some dances were performed in which lions were imitated.[116] Both Athenaeus and the Greek scholar Pollux refer to these "lion dances," and judging by the context of the references it is possible that, like the parade of wild beasts, they were held in honour of Artemis.[117]

Lastly, Alleyn Diesel's research argues that feline associations with goddesses are based more on the perceived characteristics of

---

[114] Quoted in Bevan 1985, p. 231.

[115] Wide 1973, p. 127.

[116] Ibid., p. 231.

[117] See, for example, Athenaeus 499a.

cats and their association with "virginity" than their predatorial power: "The nature and characteristics of the cat are reflected in this concept of virginity: independence, self-reliance, confident elegance and grace, prodigious sexuality, fiercely protective motherhood, and a willingness to be tamed only on its own terms, never so dependent on its domestic life that it is unable to revert to wildness."[118] As such, Artemis' connection with felines is self-explanatory. Her independence is of utmost importance, and she is without a permanent partner or companion. While she has numerous followers and attendants, Artemis is the only Olympian to have no familial or parental obligations. Athena is a close second, but Athena's commitment to Athens and the justice system, as well as her constant assistance in Athenian battles, keeps her rooted in mortal responsibilities. Artemis has no such responsibilities. She is as free as the wind, and while she may have favoured companions, she easily flows from one social connection to another. Her primary goal is independence. This explains her representation with lions and leopards rather than just cats in the way Egyptian goddesses are depicted as "cat-goddesses." Artemis is not a feline divinity. Rather, she rules and controls the mightiest of beasts, who are at her mercy and obey her demands. As Diesel argues, "The challenge, finally, of the association of felines and female divinities, is for women to re-claim that proud assertive independence epitomized by those 'virgin' deities and their feline familiars, recognizing that the image of these powerful goddesses can act as the inspiration to re-establish the sense of a sacred link between femaleness (humanity) and all nature."[119] This "virgin" feline connection is rooted in the archaic traditions that the Greek Artemis inherited as part of her mantle as "Mistress of Animals." The goddess of

[118] Diesel 2008, p. 90.
[119] Diesel 2008, p. 92.

the wild cannot be tamed, even if the Greeks try their very best to reshape her into a "maiden huntress." Even in this infantile depiction, Artemis answers to no one but lives by her own choices, creates her own justice, and acts without consulting her Olympian family. She is truly the lion of the Greek pantheon, the embodiment of true autonomy and self-sovereignty.

The Red Deer of Greece

The relationship between symbolic animal and divinity is often complex, especially when the animal is both hunted and protected by the deity, as well as sacrificed for the deity's pleasure and benevolence. Furthermore, gods will take on the shape of their close animal companions in ritual and myth, and this metamorphosis is a complicated shared spiritual experience that affects both the god and their sacred servants. The intricacy of deer symbolism, both as protected animal and ritual sacrifice, is especially and uniquely evident in Artemis' temples and sacred stories.

Artemis is depicted with deer in numerous temple reliefs, statues, and vase paintings that can be traced back to almost a millennia before the Greeks established the Olympian pantheon. Sometimes she holds these animals by their hind legs or grabs them by their necks. Her association with deer is so prolific in the ancient world that her mythos with the animal is interlinked in a way that is unlike any other Olympian divinity. One could say that the deer is her "brand," and it is unlikely that anyone living in the Mediterranean would have been ignorant of the significance this animal had to the "Lady of the Wild." In fact, even today, deer remain the domain of Artemis' stories and retelling of old myths and rituals across Greece where her worship continues to echo in the natural habitat of this majestic "king of the forest."

Homer describes Artemis as the "archer, [who] roves over the mountains, along the ridges of lofty Taygetus or Erymanthus, joying in the pursuit of boars and swift deer" (Homer, *Odyssey* 6.104). This wandering trait continues to be attributed to the goddess in artistic representations in which the deer, stag, doe, or fawn become a defining attribute. Therefore, it is unsurprising to learn that hunters often bestowed deer skin and/or antlers to the sanctuaries of Artemis as offerings of honour and sacrifice. For example, Diodorus Siculus describes the practice of hunters in Sicily hanging up deer antlers and other non-edible parts on trees, hoping for her favour (4.22). The hunter Lycormas hung up a deer skin and horns in the sanctuary of Artemis *Agrotera* in gratitude for a successful hunt,[120] and Pausanias describes the statue of Artemis in the temple of Despoine at Lycosura dressed in deerskin: "[I]t is said by the Arcadians to have seen, when dwelling in Lycosura, the sacred deer, enfeebled with age, of the goddess called Lady. This deer, they say, had a collar round its neck, with writing on the collar: 'I was a fawn when captured, at the time when Agapenor went to Troy'" (Pausanias 8.10.10). As such, the practice of donating the remains of the hunt is attested to repeatedly, and often, and the goddess seems pleased with such offerings.

While Artemis, and her dedicated hunters, pursued deer for sport and food, she is also known as a fierce protector of the animal, and many stories describe deer left to roam freely under her protection. For example, in the sanctuary of Artemis on the island of Icaria, deer were allowed to graze the sacred grounds, and no one was allowed to hunt them except as a sacrifice to the deity. Philostratus claims that in her shrines as Artemis *Agrotera* fawns also grazed untouched and unaffected.[121]

---

[120] Bevan 1985, p. 100.
[121] Bevan 1985, 112.

Artemis and her companion Taygete often assume the form of deer. Gimbutas identifies Artemis in this form as *Elaphia*, "She of the Red Deer," or *Elaphebolia*, "She Who Strikes the Red Deer." This embodiment of the "Huntress" is celebrated widely at an Attic festival of this same name, *Elaphebolia*, where Artemis receives a deer sacrifice and honey cakes in the shape of a deer.[122] This offering of *elaphoi* cakes may have been a substitute for real life victims.[123] This festival, and its namesake, is directly connected to one of the largest deer species worldwide, and the largest herbivore in Greece, the red deer (*Cervus elaphus*).[124] This breed of deer, which gets its name from the bright colour of its red fur, stands at about six feet tall (without antlers) and weighs approximately 400 pounds. In the time of Olympian worship, red deer were widespread throughout Greece, though unfortunately today herd numbers have dwindled, with many of the remaining deer finding refuge on Mount Parnitha, which is a designated national park and part of the EU's Natura 2000 network of core breeding and resting sites for rare and threatened species.[125] A smaller population also inhabits the Rhodopes Mountains in northeastern Greece. Roaming Mount Parnitha all year round, the red deer migrate to lower altitudes in search of food in the wintertime. In autumn, during breeding season, adult stags can be heard calling out for females with a bellowing cry that almost mimics a lion's roar.

While many may not consider the deer, a calm and timid animal, a tool of destruction, Artemis makes use of the animal in her schemes of vengeance or punishment, and there are numerous stories where hunters are often lured to their demise

---

[122] Ibid., p. 113.
[123] Bevan 1985, p. 101.
[124] See https://www.portesmagazine.com/red-deer-of-greece.
[125] Bevan 1985, p. 92.

by a stag. At Stymphalos, for example, huntsmen chased a fugitive deer off a cliff and drowned in the sea. Sam Wide interprets this myth as the stag being Artemis herself, luring the huntsmen, who were negligent of her worship, to their death.[126] At Saronis, Apollodorus tells us the story of Otus and Ephialtes, who planned on cornering and assaulting the goddess. Angry at their insolence, Artemis turns herself into a deer and runs between the two young men. At seeing the deer, both men shoot their arrows to kill it, and instead shoot and kill each other (Apollodorus, *Library* 1.7.4). This type of metamorphism is not limited to only Artemis herself but has been used in defence of other innocent victims, particularly young women who are being threatened by the insatiable appetites of men or male divinities. In the case of her friend Taygeta, for example, Artemis turns the young woman into a deer in order to save her from the sexual pursuit of Zeus. Once free of Zeus' advances, Taygeta returns to her human form and, in thanks for the goddess's protection, offers Artemis a deer with golden horns — the same animal Heracles would later go on to capture as part of his Twelve Labours.[127]

These stories of metamorphosis and/or shapeshifting link the divinity to her totem animal and explain why so many temple statues of Artemis are dressed in the skins of her favourite animal. It also creates a complex relationship between the natural world and the reality of the human experience. As followers of Artemis often were dressed in deer costume or symbolically "became" the deer in ritual and offerings,[128] the experience of prey as well as "protected sanctuary" was a

---

[126] Wide 1973, p. 127.

[127] See *Scholia in Pindarum Olympian Odes* 3.53.

[128] Strabo (14.643), for instance, claims that there may have been a ritual in which Artemis' priestesses donned the goddess's vestments, which consisted of a deer hide with antlers.

complicated leap of the human imagination and created both a sympathetic and ecstatic experience of the wild. This process of women "turning themselves into deer" harkens to a cross-cultural ritual of the celebration of nature and the sanctity of a birth body.

One of the ways deer rituals were celebrated was through dance. Stag dances have been performed around solstice and harvest celebrations throughout the year in England, Romania, and Germany by men dressed as women, suggesting a dance in worship of a female deity.[129] Again we see a connection between organic representation of nature through the female body and, as such, men having to perform as women in order to connect to the feminine divine. A Minoan seal from Zakros on Crete portrays a probable stag dancer with a huge antler for a head, upraised arms, and large breasts.[130] Gimbutas claims that the tradition of stag dances can be traced back to much earlier times: "At Star Carr, an early Post-Glacial camp dating from around 8000 to 7500 BCE southeast of Scarborough England, skulls of stags had been hacked into headdresses, antlers still in place, the interior of the crania smoothed, the temples punctured for thongs to be passed through."[131] Archeological research has discovered that deer portrayals or sculptures of seated women with deer antlers are recorded throughout the Bronze Age and continue into the Iron Age. As such, the interlinked relationship between the goddess, her sacred animal, her servants, and nature was a complex performance reflecting the complexities of an agricultural society deeply connected to its wild roots, and celebrating this wilderness through the physical link of the

---

[129] Ibid., p. 115.
[130] Ibid., p. 115.
[131] Ibid., p. 115.

bodies of women and a ritualistic association with the untamed and undomesticated.

She Who Hunts — and Kills

The Greek Artemis as "Huntress" has long been subjected to repeated dismissals by Classicists, who constantly cast her as a "virginal maiden in the woods" who is concerned only with her animals and her female entourage. In this tradition, she is often depicted as frolicking in the wilderness, more concerned with the welfare of her animal companions and their habitats than any worldly or political concerns in the realm of men. The Artemis described by many scholars seems more an environmentalist who is sometimes bothered by poachers and suitors than a goddess whose wrath and swift punishment should be a cause of concern.

This version of the Greek Artemis has long been a thorn in my side. As I collected more and more stories of a goddess that can be as vicious as she is caring, and as vengeful as she is protective, I realized early on that she was being purposely overlooked as a powerful divinity of righteous rage and dark vengeance. She is very clearly a goddess who kills without a second thought — a mercenary, a goddess who takes no prisoners and often offers no forgiveness, her arrows shoot to kill, and she is more fearsome than historically imagined. It is this Artemis who draws the loyalty and commitment of her followers, particularly women, as her main victims are men whose hubris is punishable by death.

Most of the male hunters killed by Artemis are caught in the act of either an attempt at sexual assault or an act of violation, such as sneaking up on the naked goddess in the woods or seducing her nymphs and priestesses. Other men boast or challenge her hunting skills and always, *absolutely always*, find themselves on the wrong end of her golden arrows. Once an attempted violation is made, Artemis has no forgiveness, and her punishment is gruesome and painful. As we will see below, many hunters who cross her are torn to pieces by wild animals, transformed into wild animals themselves and then shot and killed by their own fellow hunters or dogs, or simply terminated on the spot by the goddess's unforgiving weapon.

Punishable Offence: Against Her Mother

Traditionally, we know how steadfast Artemis is in the protection of her mother Leto. As a fundamental part of her own myth of origin, we are told that Artemis was born first and then assisted her mother in giving birth to her twin Apollo. It is no surprise that a child should defend her mother, especially a daughter. Relationships between mothers and daughters could be complicated in the Greek world, mostly due to the fact that daughters left their mothers behind once they were married; we see this represented metaphorically in the myth of Demeter and Persephone, a story so widely celebrated and honoured, it can only be viewed as evidence that the bond between women is one of the strongest familial bonds in ancient Greek society. The relationship between fathers and sons, on the other hand, is so often homicidal, the Greeks created their own term for such conflicts: *patricide*, the killing of one's father. These male conflicts within a family inevitably end with one male (often the son) replacing the other, and there are numerous legends and stories that describe the devastating relationships between fathers and their "replacements." But among stories of mothers and daughters the focus tends to be on the unbreakable bond between the women, and particularly on the devastation mothers feel when their daughters are "taken away" from them when they are married off by their fathers or uncles.

Artemis, however, is the daughter who never leaves her mother. There are only two mother–daughter relationships in the official Olympian pantheon: Demeter and Persephone, and Leto and Artemis. Unlike Persephone, Artemis is neither taken by another god or male suitor, nor does she ever "leave" her mother under the brunt, or duty, of patriarchy. As such, the relationship between Artemis and her mother is unique, and the position that Artemis takes as bodyguard/protector/defender is clear in the numerous stories in which anyone who hurts or offends her mother is harshly dispatched. Artemis is not just a daughter but is the epitome of daughters. She sets the bar of familial loyalty and is judge and executioner of anyone, man or woman, who attempts to violate or insult her parent or family.

There are several stories of men who attempt to harm Leto while she is pregnant with the twins. In southern Greece, for instance, Leimon, an Arcadian man, convinces his people to expel the pregnant goddess Leto when she comes to their land seeking refuge. Later, Artemis and her brother return to Arcadia seeking to avenge their mother, and, out of fear of accusation, Leimon kills his own brother in an attempt to save himself from the twins' vengeance. Artemis, seeing his blatant guilt, is so enraged with his arrogance and his heartlessness in the treatment of her mother, that she strikes him down with her deadly arrows:

> Apollo and Artemis, they say, throughout every land visited with punishment all the men of that time who, when Leto was with child and in the course of her wanderings, took no heed of her when she came to their land. So when the divinities came to the

land of Tegea, Skephros, they say, the son of Tegeates, came to Apollo and had a private conversation with him. And Leimon, who also was a son of Tegeates, suspecting that the conversation of Skephros contained a charge against him, rushed on his brother and killed him. Immediate punishment for the murder overtook Leimon, for he was shot by Artemis. (Pausanias 8.53.1)

Leto had a hard time finding a place to rest and give birth to the twins. On some level, this story of looking for a safe space to birth two saviour gods is echoed later in the story of the Virgin Mary looking for shelter to give birth to her saviour son, Jesus. In her search, Leto is continually pursued by a giant dragon-serpent, Python of Phocis. He was known for being the guardian of Delphi, and this myth is a patriarchal attempt to destroy the relationship between the divine feminine and serpents in the same way this relationship is permanently severed in the biblical story of Eve and Adam. After their birth, Artemis and her twin exact revenge on the serpent by slaying the monster with their arrows. Most versions, however, say that it was Apollo alone who slew the beast,[132] which is no surprise when we contextualize this myth as patriarchal propaganda. Once the dragon-serpent was slain, the people of Corinth turned against Artemis and Apollo by trying to send them away when the pair came seeking purification. The twin gods were so enraged that they brought a deadly plague down on the city until, appeased by the supplications of seven youths

---

[132] See, for example, Pseudo-Hyginus, *Fabulae* 140.

and seven maidens, they relinquished their punishment and left the people of Corinth to dwell in peace.[133]

In another story, the giant Tityos saw Leto, as she was passing through his region (Pytho) and attempted to rape the goddess. She called out to her twin children, who rushed to her rescue and killed the giant with their arrows, dispatching him to Hades and eternal torture as punishment for the crime: "Tityos saw Leto when she came to Pytho and in a fit of passion tried to embrace her. But she called out to her children, who shot him dead with arrows. He is being punished even in death, for vultures feast on his heart in Hades' realm" (Apollodorus, *Library* 1.22). In addition, Pindar tells us that Artemis sentences Tityos to an eternity of torture and pain as a lesson to all men who dare to rape women or seduce them without consent: "Tityos by Artemis was hunted down with darts from her unconquerable quiver suddenly sped [for attempting to rape her mother], so that a man may learn to touch only those loves that are within his power" (Pindar, *Pythian Ode* 4.4). It is a wonder this story has not been more easily and repeatedly accessed by modern scholars, especially in a time when consent plays such a pivotal role in the education of young people on sexual assault. Artemis is a goddess that protects against rape, but who also punishes male perpetrators for the very act of taking a woman's body without her expressed permission. As such, Artemis can be described as feminist divinity, long before this terminology or categorization of women activists was part of societal vernacular. By not acknowledging the wrath and vengeance of Artemis, scholars continue to ignore the plight of women at the hands of men in ancient Greek culture. To be fair, the issue of rape and physical assault has been recently debated by some classical scholars, but the figure of Artemis as

---

[133] Pausanias 2.7.6.

purposeful protector against these violations has been mostly relegated to footnotes and/or short abbreviations.

Punishable Offense: Consent and Intent

Much of Artemis' wrath revolves around being defiled by the male gaze. Many of her vengeance myths describe male hunters who sneak up on the goddess to get an unpermitted glimpse of her naked body. For example, the story of Actaeon, a young prince and hunter of Thebes in Boeotia who incurred the wrath of Artemis by spying on her as she bathed, is terrifying in its cruelty and gruesome details. Though some say he came across Artemis by accident, the young man nevertheless failed to avert his gaze, and this voyeuristic violation was met with swift and terrible punishment. Artemis transformed young Actaeon into the very thing he was hunting, a stag, and then incited his loyal hounds to tear him apart in a mad frenzy. Several ancient writers give accounts of this well-known tale of revenge and punishment, but Ovid's is the most vivid in describing Actaeon's suffering at the teeth and claws of his hounds and the cheering of Actaeon's hunting friends:

> They [the dogs] held their master down till the whole pack, united, sank their teeth into his flesh. He gave a wailing scream, not human, yet a sound no stag could voice, and filled with anguished cries the mountainside he knew so well; then, suppliant on his knees, turned his head silently from side to side, like arms that turned and pleaded. But his friends with their glad usual shouts cheered on the pack, not knowing what they did, and looked around

to find Actaeon; each louder than the rest
calling Actaeon, as though he were not there;
and blamed his absence and his sloth that
missed the excitement of the kill. Hearing his
name, he turned his head. Would that he were
indeed absent! But he was there. Would that he
watched, not felt, the hounds' fierce savagery!
Now they are all around him, tearing deep
their master's flesh, the stag that is no stag;
and not until so many countless wounds had
drained away his lifeblood, was the wrath, it's
said, of chaste Diana [Artemis] satisfied. (Ovid,
Metamorphoses 3.138 ff)

The metaphorical significance of this myth is often overlooked
in favour of the story's more gruesome features. It is not just
that the young hunter is torn apart by the very tools (dogs) he
has trained and brought with him to tear apart his prey, but the
fact that the hunter becomes the hunted due to his inappropriate
gaze at the naked body of a woman/goddess. This young man
feels the violation, *feels* the vulnerability as prey, and experiences
the violence of attracting unwanted attention. This myth is
profound in its expression of victim psychology, particularly the
vulnerability women experience on a daily basis for simply being
in their bodies and gazed upon as like prey. As such, Actaeon
experiences the helplessness of being a body of prey firsthand,
held against this will and hearing the cheering of his friends
before being torn apart by those he trained for his own protection.

It is unclear why Actaeon suffered so severely while others like
Orion and Buphagus, who attempted to rape the goddess, were
killed immediately and without transformation or humiliation.
Orion, a giant of Crete was slain by Artemis either because he

boasted to be superior to the goddess in hunting, or because he attempted to rape the goddess or one of her companions.[134] Buphagus, an Arcadian man from southern Greece, attempted to rape the goddess who, in her wrath, struck him down with deadly arrows.[135] Perhaps the nature of the violation, measured against the offence, led to a swift death sentence rather than a torturous one? While Orion and Buphagus may have intended to rape Artemis, the fact that Actaeon was in a position to *view* that which is unviewable by a mortal man was more of a crime and deserved a crueler punishment; his crime was more of action (seeing) rather than only intent (wanting).

Punishable Offence: Male Hunters and Their Hubris

Other men, kings and hunters alike, faced retribution for offending the goddess with their arrogance or lack of honour. Oeneus, a king of Calydon in Aetolia, neglected Artemis in his dedication of the first fruits of the seasons to the gods. In her wrath, the goddess sent a giant boar to ravage his lands, destroying crops and slaying peasants. When the boar was killed by Prince Meleager and his band of heroes, she incited conflict among the hunters, igniting a war between the Calydonians and the neighbouring Curetes tribe.[136] Forgetting Artemis after a successful hunt or harvest was not wise, and the goddess found innumerable ways to express her anger. When Admetus, a king of Pherae in Thessaly forgot to offer Artemis her dues in his matrimonial sacrifices, she filled his bridal chambers with coiled serpents.[137] But perhaps one of the most interesting

---

[134] Pseudo-Apollodorus, *Bibliotheca* 1. 25.

[135] Pausanias 8. 27. 17.

[136] Pseudo-Apollodorus, *Bibliotheca* 1. 66.

[137] Pseudo-Apollodorus, *Bibliotheca* 1. 105.

stories of hubris is that of Atreus, the king of Mycenae in the Argolis, father of Agamemnon under whom Greeks fought in the Trojan War. According to legend, Atreus had promised to sacrifice the best sheep in his herd to Artemis but failed to do so when he realized a golden lamb was born; in his greed, he kept the lamb for himself. The goddess inflicted punishment on his son Agamemnon by sending storms (or, some say, calm waters) to prevent the Greek fleet from sailing to Troy. While we have seen in previous chapters that there are stories that claim that Agamemnon himself earns Artemis' wrath by shooting one of her deer while hunting, it is interesting to note that a similar legend evolved around his father. It seems both father and son suffered from an insatiable drive to prove themselves better than the gods and, as a result, both suffer greatly at the hands of the Olympians.

Transgressions of hubris against the goddess include many made by young men who boasted they were more skilled at the art of the hunt than the "Lady of the Wild" herself. Such brazen challenges were met with terrible consequences meant to humble and chastise anyone who dared to compared themselves to an Olympian of Artemis' calibre. Broteas, a prince of Lydia (in Asia Minor), incurred the wrath Artemis, which led to his demise. He was a skilled hunter who scorned the goddess, perhaps even boasting that he was superior to her in hunting, and as punishment Artemis drove him mad, causing him to throw himself into a fire.[138] Death was often the result of human boasting, and the goddess was merciless in her contempt for such behaviour. Anceaus is another hunting prince who paid with his life for claiming that not even Artemis could prevent him from slaying the Calydonian Boar. A prince of Arcadia, Anceaus was killed by the very boar he hunted as Artemis'

---

[138] Pseudo-Apollodorus, *Bibliotheca* E2. 2

wrath drove the animal to tear the young man to pieces with its massive tusks.[139] Not only did Artemis exact her vengeance quickly and without remorse, but she also enjoyed the irony of punishing humans with the very source of their overconfidence. Another young man who fell to the tusks of a wild boar at the command of the goddess was Adonis. A prince and hunter of the island of Cyprus in the Eastern Mediterranean, Adonis has a complicated history with several Olympian goddesses and is a favourite of Aphrodite. His story, originally told to us by Hesiod, is as follows:

> Hesiod says that he was the son of Phoinix and Alphesiboia; but Panyassis calls him the son of Theias, king of the Assyrians, whose daughter was Smyrna. Because of Aphrodite's wrath (for she did not honour Aphrodite), Smyrna developed a lust for her father, and with the help of her nurse slept with him for twelve nights without his knowing it. When he found out he drew his sword and started after her, and as he was about to overtake her, she prayed to the gods to become invisible. The gods took pity on her and changed her into the tree called the Smyrna. Nine months later the tree split open and the baby named Adonis was born. Because of his beauty, Aphrodite secreted him away in a chest, keeping it from the gods, and left him with Persephone. But when Persephone got a glimpse of Adonis, she refused to return him. When the matter was brought to Zeus for arbitration, he divided the year into three

[139] Ovid, *Metamorphoses* 8. 269

parts and decreed that Adonis would spend
one third of the year by himself, one third
with Persephone, and the rest with Aphrodite.
(Apollodorus, *Library* 3.183)

Despite his being favoured by so many Olympian gods, or perhaps because of it, Adonis offends Artemis with his boasts of superior hunting prowess and is slain without clemency by the goddess in a similar fashion to others before him: "While Adonis was still a boy, because of Artemis' anger he was wounded by a boar during a hunt and died."[140] While many young men died in the hunt for deer and boars, the fact that these deaths were attributed to the goddess Artemis, particularly in response to the egotism of the hunters, is often cast aside as a side note or an explanation for hunting accidents. However, the fact that Artemis is responsible for such vengeful slayings speaks to her ancestry as "Mistress of Animals," a goddess of the wild, a divine feminine to be respected and feared by mortals, especially while in her domain of forests and wild beasts.

Punishable Offence: Women and Vanity

The capital punishment for boasting is not limited to men. Artemis is equally harsh with women who indulge their vanity or who forget to keep their commitment to her worship. Several stories of the goddess' wrath and punishment of women serve as a warning for women who think themselves beyond her anger. For example, the fate of Euthemia, a young nymph who was struck down by the arrows of Artemis for her lack of reverence,

---

[140] Pseudo-Apollodorus, *Bibliotheca* 3. 183

is evidence that the goddess is stern in the discipline of even her most favoured companions:

> Meropes, who ruled the island of Cos ... had a wife, Euthemia, of the race of nymphs, who was stuck with the arrows of [Artemis] when she ceased worshipping her. At last, she was snatched away alive by [Persephone] to the Land of the Dead. Meropes, moved by longing for his wife, would have committed suicide, but [Hera], pitying him, changed him into an eagle. (Hyginus, *Astronomica* 2.16)

This story is particularly significant because it shows almost all the other Olympian goddesses acting more merciful than Artemis and her deadly arrows. While Euthemia gained favour with Persephone and Hera, she was not able to survive Artemis' retribution.

In another story, in a moment of self indulgence, Chione, who was loved (or the lover) of both Apollo and Hermes, speaks harshly of Artemis during a hunt and is consequently slain by her arrows.[141] According to Ovid, Chione may have even boasted of her beauty when comparing herself to the goddess, and this vanity cost the girl her life:

> She [Chione] dared to set herself above [Artemis], faulting her fair face. The goddess, fierce in fury, cried "You'll like my actions better!" and she bent her bow and shot her arrow, and the shaft transfixed that tongue that well deserved it [for her sacrilege]. Then

---

[141] Hyginus, *Fabulae* 200.

that tongue was dumb, speech failed the words
she tried to say: her blood and life ebbed away.
(Ovid, *Metamorphoses* 11.321)

While goddesses are known for disciplining anyone who speaks in a disrespectful way, it is important to note that this is another example of Artemis not making any expectations for those favoured by other members of her divine family. She did not forgive Adonis who was especially favoured by Aphrodite and Persephone, and she killed Chione without mercy, even though she was a favourite of her twin brother and Hermes. As such, Artemis is a goddess to be both feared and revered. She is not a "pure virgin," nor is she depicted as a kind or gentle one-dimensional protectress. While we have seen her in the role of "Saviour" and "Protector," she is equally as vicious and merciless as she is kind.

Perhaps the most devastating story of Artemis' wrath is the story of Niobe and her fourteen children.[142] Niobe was the queen of Thebes in Boeotia, and she was excessively proud of her fourteen children and claimed superiority in motherhood over the goddess Leto. When Apollo and Artemis, Leto's children, heard Niobe's insolent bragging, they rushed to their mother's defense and descended on Thebes to punish Niobe and strike down her children with their arrows:

> Amphion married Niobe, the daughter of
> Tantalus, who bore him seven sons ... and as
> many daughters ... With her fine brood Niobe

---

[142] Homer claims there were twelve children (*Iliad* 24.602), but according to Weir Smyth, "Sources other than the text inform us that Aeschylus gave Niobe fourteen children, a number adopted by Euripides and Aristophanes."

claimed to be more blest with children than Leto. Leto was annoyed by this and urged Artemis and Apollo against Niobe's children. Artemis killed all the females in the house with her arrows, and Apollo all the males as they were hunting together on Mount [Cithaeron]. Of the males only Amphion was spared, and of the females only Chloris the Elder, whom Neleus married. According to Telesilla, Amyclas and Meliboea were spared, and Amphion was shot down by them. As for Niobe, she left Thebes and went to her father Tantalus at Sipylus, where, after a prayer to Zeus, her form was turned to stone, from which tears flow by night and by day. (Pseudo-Apollodorus, *Bibliotheca* 3. 46)

Pausanias tells us that Amyclas was spared from the mercenary twins because he prayed to Leto who took pity on the youngest children: "When the children of Amphion were destroyed by Apollo and Artemis, she [Chloris] alone of her sisters, along with Amyclas escaped; their escape was due to their prayers to Leto" (Pausanias 2.21.9). This account might be Pausanias' explanation for why Aeschylus and others claim that fourteen children were killed, while Homer states that it was twelve. Either way, this story is shocking for anyone who views Artemis as only a kind and forgiving goddess. As the goddess of childbirth, and often the protector of mothers and their young, it is almost unfathomable to imagine Artemis killing the innocent daughters of Niobe on the command of her mother. It challenges the view that the "Lady of the Wild" was a benevolent goddess who frolicked freely with her deer in the forests and bathed with her nymphs in rivers and warm lakes. This story, famously reproduced in art and literature for millennia, is a reminder that Artemis has darker and more archaic roots. It harkens back to the time of Gorgons and Furies and women who did not shy away from "unpleasant" responsibilities of survival and discipline. It connects the goddess with an undercurrent of cold and methodical duty and complicates much of her more compassionate myths. It also reminds mortals that the divine can be both "Saviour" and executioner, and that the judgement of a god does not necessarily evolve around kindness or forgiveness. Artemis is a goddess of deep complexities and the inheritor of divine nuances many would prefer to bury under the guise of the maiden "Huntress." It is frightening to imagine that the goddess of the hunt might hunt the very mortals that offend her, and even more so, the innocents attached to said mortals, such as the children of Niobe.

We chaste girls and boys
Are under the tutelage of Diana:
Chaste boys and girls
Let us sing to Diana.

O daughter of Leto,
Great offspring of greatest Jove,
Your mother bore you
Near the Delian olive tree,

So you might be mistress of the mountains
And of the growing woods
And of the secluded woodland glades
And of the sounding rivers:

You are called Lucina Juno
By women in the pains of childbirth,
You are called powerful Trivia and
You are called Luna by your borrowed light.

You, goddess, in your monthly course
Marking off the journey of the year,
You fill up the rural hut
Of the farmer with good crops.

By whatever name pleases you
May you be hallowed,
And as you have been accustomed to before, may you
Preserve the offspring of Romulus with good aid.

- **Catullus**[143]

---

[143] Catullus. *The Carmina of Gaius Valerius Catullus*. Leonard C. Smithers. London. Smithers. 1894.

GODDESS OF TRANSITIONS: A CONCLUSION

The religion of Artemis is a complex phenomenon, similar in some ways to the various forms of Christianity, whose religious worship evolved over 2,000 years. Orthodox, Catholic, and Protestant Christianity share some features in common — myths as well as rituals — but they differ significantly as well in terms of beliefs, rituals, and their interpretation. The same is true of Artemis' worship, which shares some ritual commonalities but differs in terms of myths of origins. The religion of Artemis seems to have three distinct and overlapping identities, likely reflecting a process of adaptation as her worship was developed and modified at different times and in different areas of the Mediterranean. In one form, Artemis is the twin sister of Apollo and the daughter of Leto (e.g., *Hymn to Artemis* 9.2 and 27.3). In another aspect, she is the goddess of the nymphs of Arcadia, the mountainous, forested centre of the Peloponnese. At Tauris and Brauronia, she is found in a form where her worship at one time included human sacrifices (Euripides, *Iphigenia in Tauris* 36.). While different in their details, all these various forms reflect the worship of Artemis and testify to her popularity and sustaining power throughout various cultures of the Mediterranean. She was the deity who united cultures and peoples around her divinity and worship.

In a sense, Artemis was the first international goddess. She is the repository of all goddess attributes and images.

The evolution of the religion of Artemis extends at least as far back as predynastic Egypt, through Minoan and Mycenaean culture and on into the Greek period. It is evident from this history that Artemis is the key figure through which goddess ritual, tradition, and community worship is preserved and adapted across space and over time. By the Greek period, Artemis had likely become the most popular goddess of the Mediterranean. This popularity and the devotion of her followers is evident not only in her numerous titles and incarnations but particularly in the moments in which she is called upon or adored. Moments that begin with birth and move through the life experiences of both Greek males and females. She is as equally responsible for a successful marriage (e.g., in Brauron) as a successful battle (in Sparta), and she participates in the final transition from dying to crossing into the mysteries of the afterlife.

Artemis is a creature of margins, at home in the mountains and marshes and comfortable inside the city gates. If we consider the forests and mountains as a representation of childish abandon and wildness, and the economies and politics of cities as a representation of adulthood, then we can agree with Redfield, who argues that the setting of myth, as well as the place of ritual, is largely metaphorical. As a result of this metaphorical logic of myth, Artemis presides over the boundary between child and adult, and is often patroness of initiations.[144] The initiations for both males and females that Artemis oversees with a severe discipline are fundamental to Greek life. The coming-of-age ritual is an event without which Greek citizens could not move forward and become successful in their respective responsibilities. Redfield states that every

---

[144] Redfield 1990, p. 129.

ritual symbolizes and strengthens the community that it helps to connect. The specific content of the ritual further defines that community.[145] The ritual authenticates the transition of the individual and allows the community to come together in the acceptance of the individual's new identity. Clearly, Artemis is the only goddess of the traditional Greek pantheon who can command both order and prestige in this practice. Her attributes, which encompass her nurturing, kindness, and mercy, her discipline and chastity, as well as her vengeful nature, assure the community that the rituals in which they participate are both familial and political.

Artemis is also a goddess of totality. In many aspects, she is the "Saviour" (*Sôteira*), the "Bringer of Light" (*Phosphorus*), and "She Who Soothes" (*Hêmerasia*). In others, she is *Agrotera* ("Huntress") and *Iokheaira* ("Of Showering Arrows"), who rigorously protects her chastity as "Maiden" (*Parthenos*) and even "Revered Virgin" (*Aedoeus Parthenos*). Most importantly, she *Basileis* ("Royal Princess"), a goddess "Of the First Throne" (*Protothronia*) who reigns unmatched throughout the Mediterranean as "Goddess Queen" (*Potnia Thea*). This multitude of titles, attributes, and incarnations is a reflection of Artemis' constant adaptation and provides more than sufficient evidence that Artemis is a goddess for all peoples in all places: Her cult worship is as varied as the people who devote themselves to her. This diversity reflects the goddess' sphere of influence as both the agent through which community history is inherited, as well as the medium through which community culture is maintained. Her devotees are not part of a uniform cult that is simply transported from one place to another, from one time to another; rather, an array of various forms of worship are

---

[145] Ibid., p. 132.

embedded within each locality, and its unique cultural practices all fall under the aegis of Artemis.

Thus, as we have seen, Artemis, the much overlooked goddess of antiquity, transformed the Mediterranean world. She absorbed many previous goddess cults and subsumed them under her huge umbrella of attributes and forms. She transcended cultures, uniting worshippers in one religious tradition across many nations without tying them down to a rigid belief system. The worship of Artemis was an international religion. Her theology was fluid and elastic, and this enabled her to embrace various ways of thinking about the divine feminine without commanding orthodoxy or creedal formulations. Above all, she was a goddess of human transitions, offering people a way to understand and celebrate key periods of change throughout their lives, from birth to death … and perhaps beyond.

WORKS CITED

Primary Sources

Aeschylus. *Aeschylus: Fragments.* Translated by Alan H. Sommerstein. Cambridge, MA: Loeb Classical Library, 2008.

Aeschylus. *Aeschylus.* Translated by Herbert Weir Smyth. Loeb Classical Library Vols. 145–146. Cambridge, MA: Harvard UP, 1926.

Aeschylus. *Prometheus Bound.* Translated by Gilbert Murray. London: George Allen & Unwin, 1931.

Aelian. *Aelian on the Characteristics of Animals.* Translated by A. F. Scholfield. Cambridge, MA: Harvard UP, 1971.

Aelius Aristides. *Aristides and the Sacred Texts.* Translated by Charles Allison Behr. Cambridge, MA: Harvard UP, 1973.

Antoninus Liberalis. *The Metamorphoses of Antoninus Liberalis: A Translation with a Commentary.* Translated by Francis Celoria. London: Routledge, 1992.

Apollodorus. *The Library*. Translated by James George Frazer. Loeb Classical Library Vols. 121–122. Cambridge, MA: Harvard UP, 2002.

Apollonius Rhodius. *Argonautica*. Translated by R. C. Seaton. Loeb Classical Library Vol. 1. London: William Heinemann, 1912.

Athenaeus. *The Deipnosophists*. Translated by Charles Burton Gulick. London: William Heinemann, 1927.

Callimachus. *Callimachus' Hymns*. Translated by Robert Schmiel. Bryn Mawr, PA: Thomas Library, Bryn Mawr College, 1984.

Callimachus, Lycophron, and Aratus. *Hymns and Epigrams*. Translated by A. W. Mair and G. R. Mair. Loeb Classical Library Vol. 129. Cambridge, MA: Harvard UP, 1921.

The Chronography of Gregory Abu'l Faraj, The Son of Aaron, The Hebrew Physician Commonly Known as Bar Hebraeus Being the First Part of His Political History of the World. Translated by Ernest A. Wallis Budge. London: Oxford UP, 1932.

Clement of Alexandria. *The Exhortation to the Greeks. The Rich Man's Salvation. To the Newly Baptized*. Translated by G. W. Butterworth. Loeb Classical Library Vol. 92. Cambridge, MA: Harvard UP, 1919.

Diodorus Siculus. *Library of History (Books III–VIII)*. Translated by C. H. Oldfather. Loeb Classical Library Vols. 303 and 340. Cambridge, MA: Harvard UP, 1935.

Ephesia Grammata. Translated by Fritz Graf. In *Brill's New Pauly*. Online edition, 2006.

Euripides. *Iphigeneia in Tauris*. Translated by Richmond Lattimore. New York: Oxford UP, 1973.

The Greek Bucolic Poets. Translated by J. M. Edmonds. Loeb Classical Library Vol. 28. Cambridge, MA: Harvard UP, 1912.

Herodotus. *Histories*. Translated by Michael A. Flower and John Marincola. Cambridge: Cambridge UP, 2002.

Hesiod. *Homeric Hymns, Epic Cycle, Homerica*. Translated by H. G. Evelyn-White. Loeb Classical Library Vol. 57. London: William Heinemann, 1914.

Hippocrates. *Hippocrates*. Translated by W. H. S. Jones and Paul Potter. London: William Heinemann, 1923.

Homer. *The Iliad*. 2 vols. Translated by A. T. Murray. Loeb Classical Library. London: William Heinemann, 1924–5.

Homer. *The Odyssey*. Translated by A. T. Murray. Loeb Classical Library. London: William Heinemann, 1919.

The Homeric Hymns. Translated by Apostolos N. Athanassakis. Baltimore: Johns Hopkins UP, 1976.

Hyginus. *The Myths of Hyginus*. Translated by Mary A. Grant. Lawrence: U of Kansas P, 1960.

The Hymns of Orpheus. Translated by Thomas Taylor. Philadelphia: U of Pennsylvania P, 1999.

Lucian. *Selected Dialogues*. Translated by C. D. N. Costa. Oxford: Oxford UP, 2005.

Nonnus. *Dionysiaca*. Translated by W. H. D. Rouse. Loeb Classical Library Vols. 344, 354, and 356. Cambridge, MA: Harvard UP, 1940.

Oppian. *Halieuticks of the Nature of Fishes and Fishing of the Ancients*. Translated by William Diaper and John Jones. Oxford: Printed at the Theater, 1722.

The Orphic Hymns. Translated by Apostolos N. Athanassakis and Benjamin M. Wolkow. Baltimore: Johns Hopkins UP, 1976.

Pausanias. *Description of Greece*. Translated by W. H. S. Jones and H. A. Omerod. Loeb Classical Library. London: William Heinemann, 1918.

Philostratus the Elder, Philostratus the Younger, and Callistratus. *Philostratus (the Elder): Imagines; Philostratus the Younger: Imagines; Callistratus: Descriptions*. Translated by Arthur Fairbanks. London: Wililam Heinemann, 1931.

Pindar. *The Odes of Pindar*. Translated by Richmond Lattimore. Chicago: U of Chicago P, 1947.

Plato. *Symposium*. Translated by Benjamin Jowett in *Collected Works of Plato*, 4th ed. Oxford: Oxford UP, 1953.

Pliny the Elder. *Historia Naturalis*. Edited by Joyce Irene Whalley. London: Sidwick & Jackson, 1982.

Plutarch. *Moralia*. Translated by Frank Cole Babbitt. Cambridge, MA: Harvard UP, 1931.

Sophocles. *The Ajax of Sophocles*. Edited by Sir Richard Jebb. Cambridge: Cambridge UP, 1893.

Strabo. *The Geography of Strabo*. Translated by Hans Claude Hamilton and W. Falconer. London: G. Bell & Sons, 1903.

Valerius Maximus. *Memorable Deeds and Sayings*. Translated by D. Wardle. Oxford: Clarendon, 1997.

Venantius Fortunatus. *Personal and Political Poems*. Edited by Judith W. George. Liverpool: Liverpool UP, 1995.

Secondary Sources

Adams, Barbara. *Predynastic Egypt*. Princess Risborough: Shire, 1988.

Aldhelm, and Rudolf Ehwald. *Aldhelmi Opera*. Berlin: Weidmannsche Buchhandlung, 1919.

Anderson, Florence Bennett. *Religious Cults Associated with the Amazons*. New York: AMS Press, 1967.

Anderson, Pamela Sue. *A Feminist Philosophy of Religion: The Rationality and Myths of Religious Belief.* Oxford: Blackwell, 1998.

Baring, Anne, and Jules Cashford. *The Myth of the Goddess: Evolution of an Image*. London: Viking Arkana, 1991.

Beard, Mary, and John A. North. *Pagan Priests: Religion and Power in the Ancient World*. London: Duckworth, 1990.

Bell, C. "The Ritual Body and the Dynamics of Ritual Power." *Journal of Ritual Studies* 4, no. 2 (Summer 1990): 299–313.

Benard, Elisabeth Anne, and Beverly Ann Moon. *Goddesses Who Rule*. New York: Oxford UP, 2000.

Berger, Pamela C. *The Goddess Obscured: Transformation of the Grain Protectress from Goddess to Saint*. Boston: Beacon Press, 1985.

Bestor, Thomas Wheaton. "Plato's Semantics and Plato's *Cratylus*." *Phronesis: A Journal for Ancient Philosophy* 25, no. 3 (1980): 306–330.

Bevan, E., 1986. *Representations of Animals in Sanctuaries of Artemis and other Olympian Deities*. Oxford: B.A.R.

Birnbaum, Lucia Chiavola. *Black Madonnas*. Palomar, 1997.

Boslooper, Thomas D. *The Virgin Birth*. Philadelphia: Westminster Press, 1962.

Budge, Ernest A. Wallis. *Miscellaneous Coptic Texts in the Dialect of Upper Egypt*. London: British Museum, 1915.

Budge, Ernest A. Wallis. *The Book of the Dead: The Hieroglyphic Transcript of the Papyrus of Ani*. New Hyde Park, NY: University Books, 1960.

Budin, Stephanie Lynn. *Images of Woman and Child from the Bronze Age: Reconsidering Fertility, Maternity, and Gender in the Ancient World*. Cambridge: Cambridge UP, 2011.

Burkert, Walter. *Greek Religion*. Cambridge, MA: Harvard UP, 1985.

Calame, Claude. *Choruses of Young Women in Ancient Greece: Their Morphology, Religious Role, and Social Functions*. Translated by Derek Collins and Janice Orion. Lanham, MD: Lanham and Littlefield, 1997.

Connor, W. R. "Tribes, Festivals, and Processions: Civil Ceremonial and Political Manipulation in Archaic Greece." *The Journal of Hellenic Studies* 107 (November 1987): 40–50.

Conway, D. J. *Maiden, Mother, Crone: The Myth and Reality of the Triple Goddess*. St. Paul, MN: Llewellyn Publications, 1994.

Cunneen, Sally. *In Search of Mary: The Woman and the Symbol*. New York: Ballantine Books, 1996.

Cunneen, Sally. "Breaking Mary's Silence: A Feminist Reflection on Marian Piety." *Theology Today* 56, no. 3 (October 1999): 319–335.

Davison, Peter. "Artemis." Poetry 98, no. 4 (July 1961): 209.

D'Este, Sorita. *Artemis: Virgin Goddess of the Sun and Moon*. London: Avalonia, 2005.

Diesel, Alleyn. "Felines and Female Divinities: The Association of Cats with Goddesses, Ancient and Contemporary." *Journal for the Study of Religion* Vol. 21, No. 1 (2008), pp. 71-94

Dowden, Ken. *Religion And The Romans*. Bristol Classical Press, 1995.

Downing, Christine. *The Goddess: Mythological Images of the Feminine*. New York: Continuum, 1996.

Eller, Cynthia. *Living In The Lap Of The Goddess*. Beacon Press, 1995.

Elderkin, George W., Richard Stillwell, Frederick O. Waage, Dorothy B. Waage, and Jean Lassus. *Antioch-on-the-Orontes*. Princeton: Princeton UP, 1934.

Eisler, Riane. *The Chalice and The Blade*. San Francisco: HarperSanFrancisco, 1998.

Emery, Walter B. *Archaic Egypt*. Baltimore: Penguin, 1961.

Erman, Adolf. *A Handbook of Egyptian Religion*. Translated by A. S. Griffith. London: Archibald Constable, 1907.

Farnell, Lewis Richard. *Greek Hero Cults and Ideas of Immortality: The Gifford Lectures Delivered in the University of St. Andrews in the Year 1920*. Oxford: Clarendon, 1921.

Farnell, Lewis Richard. *The Cults of the Greek States*. 5 vols. New Rochelle, NY: Clarendon, 1977.

Feininger, Andreas, and J. Bon. *The Image of Woman: Women in Sculpture from Pre-historic Times to the Present Day.* London: Thames and Hudson, 1960.

Frymer-Kensky, Tikva. *In the Wake of the Goddesses: Women, Culture, and the Biblical Transformation of Pagan Myth.* New York: Free Press, 1992.

Gadon, Elinor W. *The Once And Future Goddess.* Thorsons, 1995.

Getty, Adele. *Goddess.* Thames And Hudson, 1990.

Gimbutas, Marija. *The Gods And Goddesses Of Old Europe: 7000 To 3500 BC Myths, Legends And Cult Images.* University Of California Press, 1974.

Gimbutas, Marija. *The Language Of The Goddess.* Harpersanfrancisco, 1991.

Griffiths, Fiona J. *The Garden of Delights, Reform and Renaissance for Women in the Twelfth Century.* Philadelphia: U of Pennsylvania P, 2007.

Goldenberg, Naomi R. *Changing of the Gods: Feminism and the End of Traditional Religions.* Boston: Beacon Press, 1979.

Guthrie, Williams Keith Chambers. *A History of Greek Philosophy.* Cambridge: Cambridge UP, 1967.

Hamilton, Richard. "Alkman and the Athenian Arkteia." *Hesperia* 58, no. 4 (1989): 449–472.

Hardwick, Lorna. "Ancient Amazons: Heroes, Outsiders or Women?" *Greece & Rome* 37, no. 1 (April 1990): 14–36.

Harrison, E. Jane. *Prolegomena to the Study of Greek Religion.* pp. xxii + 674. Cambridge University Press, 1903. 15s.

Hollis, Susan Tower. "Five Egyptian Goddesses in the Third Millennium BC." *KMT: A Modern Journal of Ancient Egypt* 5, no. 4 (Winter 1994–5): 46–51.

Houghton, Valerie Lynn. *Apollonius Rhodius' Argonautica: The Feminine Principle.* PhD diss., University of Michigan, 1987.

James, Vanessa. *The Genealogy of Greek Mythology: An Illustrated Family Tree of Greek Myth from the First Gods to the Founders of Rome.* New York: Penguin, 2003.

Kees, Hermann, and T. G. Henry James. *Ancient Egypt.* University Of Chicago Press, 1961.

Kerényi, Karl. *Eleusis: Archetypal Image of Mother and Daughter.* London: Routledge & Paul, 1967.

King, H. "Bound to Bleed: Artemis and Greek Women." In *Images of Women in Antiquity,* edited by Averil Cameron and Amélie Kuhrt, 109–127. London: Routledge, 1993

Knibbe, Dieter. "*Via Sacra Ephesiaca*: New Aspects of the Cult of Artemis Ephesia." In *Ephesos, Metropolis of Asia: An Interdisciplinary Approach to Its Archaeology, Religion, and Culture,* edited by Helmut Koester, 141–155. Valley Forge, PA: Trinity Press International, 1995.

Larson, Jennifer. "Handmaidens of Artemis?" *The Classical Journal* 92, no. 3 (1997): 249–257.

Lesko, Barbara S. *The Great Goddesses of Egypt*. Norman: U of Oklahoma P, 1999.

Lesser, Rachel. "The Nature of Artemis Ephesia." *Hirundo: The McGill Journal of Classical Studies* 4 (2005–6): 43–54.

Lethaby, W. R. "The Earlier Temple of Artemis at Ephesus." *The Journal of Hellenic Studies* 37 (1917): 1–16.

Lichtheim, Miriam. *Ancient Egyptian Literature: A Book of Readings*. Berkeley: U of California P, 1973.

Lloyd-Jones, Hugh. "Artemis And Iphigeneia". *The Journal Of Hellenic Studies*, vol 103, 1983, pp. 87-102. Cambridge University Press (CUP), https://doi.org/10.2307/630530.

Maas, Anthony. "The Blessed Virgin Mary." In *The Catholic Encyclopedia* Vol. 15. New York: Robert Appleton Company, 1912. May 28, 2015, http://www.newadvent.org/cathen/15464b.htm.

MacLaurin, E. C. B. "The Canaanite Background of the Doctrine of the Virgin Mary." *Religious Traditions* 3, no. 2 (1980): 1–11.

Marinatos, N. "Goddess and Monster: An Investigation of Artemis." In *Ansichten griechischer Rituale*, 114–125. Stuttgart: Teubner, 1998.

Marinatos, Nanno. *Minoan Religion*. University Of South Carolina Press, 1993.

Moon, Warren G. *Ancient Greek Art and Iconography*. Madison: U of Wisconsin P, 1983.

Myres, J. L. "The History of the Pelasgian Theory." *The Journal of Hellenistic Studies* 27 (1907): 170–225.

Nicholson, Oliver. *The Oxford Dictionary Of Late Antiquity*. Oxford University Press, 2018.

Nilsson, Martin P. *The Mycenaean Origin of Greek Mythology*. New York: W. W. Norton, 1932.

Nilsson, Martin P. *Greek Folk Religion*. Gloucester, MA: Peter Smith, 1971.

Nilsson, Martin P. *The Minoan-Mycenaean Religion and Its Survival in Greek Religion*, 2nd rev. ed. New York: Biblo and Tannen, 1971.

Olson, Carl. *The Book of the Goddess, Past and Present: An Introduction to Her Religion*. Prospect Heights, IL: Waveland, 2002.

Papadimitriou, John. "The Sanctuary of Artemis at Brauron." *Scientific American* 208, no. 6 (1963): 110–122.

Paris, Ginette. *Pagan Meditations: The Worlds of Aphrodite, Artemis, and Hestia*. Dallas: Spring Publications, 1986.

Parke, Herbert William. *Festivals Of The Athenians*. Cornell Univ. Press, 1994.

Petrie, William. M. Flinders, and Francis Llewellyn Griffith. *The Royal Tombs of the Earliest Dynasties.* London: Egypt Exploration Fund, 1901.

Pomeroy, Sarah B. *Goddesses, Whores, Wives and Slaves. Women in Classical Antiquity.* New York: Schocken Books, 1995.

Pratt, Annis. *Dancing With Goddesses.* Netlibrary, Inc., 1999.

Price, M. *The Seven Wonders of the Ancient World.* London: Routledge, 1996.

Redfield, James. "From Sex to Politics: The Rites of Artemis Triklaria and Dionysus Aisymnētēs at Patras." In *Before Sexuality: The Construction of Erotic Experience in the Ancient Greek World,* edited by David M. Halperin, John J. Winkler, and Froma I. Zeitlin, 115–134. Princeton: Princeton UP, 1990.

Rigoglioso, Marguerite. *The Cult of Divine Birth in Ancient Greece.* New York: Palgrave Macmillan, 2009.

Roller, Lynn E. *In Search of God the Mother: The Cult of Anatolian Cybele.* Berkeley: U of California P, 1999.

Ruether, Rosemary R. *Goddesses and the Divine Feminine: A Western Religious History.* Berkeley: U of California P, 2005.

Saayman, F. "The Wrath of Artemis (and Menis!) in Ag. 122-159." *Akroterion* 39, no. 1 (1994): 2–11.

Saradi-Mendelovici, Helen. "Christian Attitudes towards Pagan Monuments in Late Antiquity and Their Legacy in Later

Byzantine Centuries." *Dumbarton Oaks Papers* 44 (1990): 47–61.

Sayed, Ramadan el-. *La deese Neith de Sais: Importance et rayonnement de son cult*. Cairo: IFAO, 1982.

Simpson, Elizabeth. "Phrygian Furniture from Gordion." In *The Furniture of Western Asia, Ancient and Traditional*, edited by Georgina Herrmann, 198–201. Mainz: Philipp von Zabern, 1996.

Sissa, Giulia. *Greek Virginity*. Cambridge, MA: Harvard UP, 1990.

Smith, William. *Dictionary of Greek and Roman Biography and Mythology*. London: J. Murray, 1849.

Thompson, G. *The Arkoudiotissa*. Kretika Chronika 15-16, pt. 3:93-96.

Thomas, Christine. "At Home in the City of Artemis: Religion in Ephesus in the Literary Imagination of the Roman Period." In *Ephesos, Metropolis of Asia: An Interdisciplinary Approach to Its Archaeology, Religion, and Culture*, edited by Helmut Koester, 81–117. Valley Forge, PA: Trinity Press International, 1995.

Velde, B., and Isabelle C. Druc. *Archaeological Ceramic Materials: Origin and Utilization*. Berlin: Springer, 1999.

Vermaseren, M. J., and Eugene Lane. *Cybele, Attis, and Related Cults: Essays in Memory of M. J. Vermaseren*. Leiden: Brill, 1996.

Walbank, M. B. "Artemis Bear-Leader." *Classical Quarterly* 31 (1986): 276–281. Wolfram, Herwig. *History of the Goths.* Translated by Thomas J. Dunlap. Berkeley: U of California P, 1988.

Wide, Sam. *Lakonische Kulte.* Wissenschaftliche Buchgesellschaft, 1973.

Zaidman, Louise. B., and Pauline S. Pantel. *Religion in the Ancient Greek City.* Cambridge: Cambridge UP, 1992.